A **CREATIVE** Approach to the Classical Progymnasmata

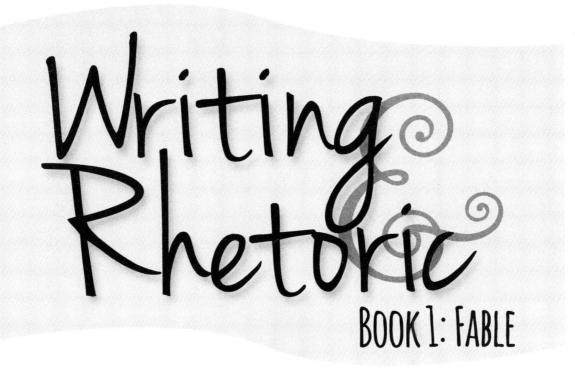

Writing & Rhetoric

Book 1: Fable

Paul Kortepeter

Writing & Rhetoric Book 1: Fable
© Classical Academic Press, 2013
Version 1.1

ISBN: 978-1-60051-216-2

Classical Academic Press
515 S. 32nd Street
Camp Hill, PA 17011

www.ClassicalAcademicPress.com

Series content editor: Christine Perrin
Series editor: Gretchen Nesbit
Illustrations: Jason Rayner
Book design: Karen Brightbill
Speech bubble icon courtesy of frankdesign/Vecteezy.com.

PGP.01.19

Fable

TABLE OF CONTENTS

A Typical Teaching Week

Veteran teachers know that rarely is there anything typical about a teaching week. These guidelines are intended to help bring some predictability to lesson planning. Although the parts of speech and other elements of grammar are important aspects of this course, its primary focus is writing and rhetoric—as the name implies. It is recommended that teachers alternate between a course in grammar one week and *Writing & Rhetoric: Fable* the next week.

Day One

1. The teacher models fluency by reading the text aloud while students follow along silently.

2. Students break off into pairs and reread the text to each other. In the case of longer fables, students can read in sections. Encouragement should be given to students to read with drama and flair where appropriate.

3. "Tell It Back" (Narration) and "Talk About It" should immediately follow the reading of the text, while the fable is still fresh in the students' minds. "Talk About It" is designed to help students analyze the meaning of texts and to see analogous situations, both in the world and in their own lives. Narration, the process of "telling back," can be done in pairs or by selecting individuals to narrate to the entire class. Playacting the story from memory is another possible form of narration. (Note: Solo students can tell back the story into a recording device or to an instructor.) The process of narration is intended to improve comprehension and long-term memory.

4. "Go Deeper" comprehension exercises follow each text. They can help students better understand the selection as they work with vocabulary, main ideas, and character traits.

Day Two

1. Optional: The teacher can appoint a student or the entire class to read the text again.

2. Students then work with the text through the "Writing Time" exercises. In ancient times, at this level, the primary exercise was to summarize or amplify the length of the narrative. Other exercises include emulating a particular sentence, changing part of a story, or writing an entirely new story. Student work need not be completely original, but it should show some effort of thought.

Day Three or Four[1]

1. A time of sharing work can wrap up each lesson. In order to build confidence in public speaking, students should be encouraged to read their work aloud—either in pairs or to the entire class.

2. The "Speak It" section creates opportunities for students to recite, to playact, and to share their work aloud.

---

1. The number of days per week assigned to the lessons is four so that you have some flexibility according to the pace and level of depth that you take advantage of with your students.

Introduction to Students

We are glad you are studying writing and rhetoric and we think you will be glad, too! In the Writing & Rhetoric series, we use whole stories to teach you how to write. First you read and think about the stories, then you have the chance to rewrite them, making them longer or shorter. Eventually, after you learn how to do that, you will write your own story. By that time, your mind will be filled with characters, words, events, and even types of sentences that will help you write.

Often, when people are taught to write, they are asked to come up with material from thin air, or *ex nihilo*, which is a Latin phrase that means "out of nothing." For instance, many students return to school in the fall and are asked to write about their summer vacation. This can be fun, but we believe the best writing skills are developed when you have many ideas, words, and examples that show you a lot of ways in which other writers have written about a subject. In a way, these other writers become your writing guides. Frequently, when a writer doesn't have such a guide, he or she gets frustrated. Even famous writers have had such guides—often their work resembles the writing style of their teachers or guides.

Now, let's get writing!

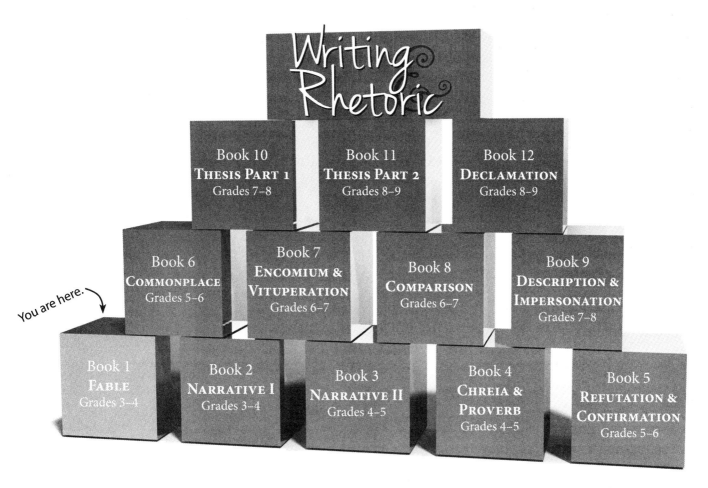

The Writing & Rhetoric series provides students with forms and models of excellent writing that students can imitate on their path to masterful writing. The first book in the series recovers this proven method of teaching writing, using fables to teach beginning writers the craft of writing well.

This is the first in a series of twelve books that will train students over six years, starting in grades three or four and up.

Introduction

Writing Happily

Where We Are Now

When it comes to writing, some students see the process as sweet delight. That was my experience. I always loved taking a blank sheet of paper and transforming it into something magical: a carnival twinkling in the night, a city street shining with rain and reflecting gas lamps, an avalanche flying down a spire of rock. But I know that writing is not a magical world for many children or even some adults.

When I served as a writing instructor at the University of Southern California (USC), I saw firsthand the failure of writing instruction at our primary and secondary schools. Hardly a day went by that I wasn't grading a stack of papers, and the torment, the agony, of writing seemed to writhe through the pages.

Many of those college students had difficulty writing grammatically correct and coherent paragraphs—let alone entire essays, persuasively written. These were smart students from privileged backgrounds. So how did they get to college with such meager writing skills? What was happening in school or at home to sabotage the development of writing? Something was clearly not working.

Some years after teaching at USC, I helped to establish The Oaks Academy in the inner city of Indianapolis. Our school has grown from a modest fifty students in 1998 to 400-plus students today. At The Oaks, our mission is "to provide a rich, classical education to children of diverse racial and socioeconomic backgrounds." Our diversity includes children who grow up in highly involved families as well as children who have limited access to opportunity and must often fend for themselves academically.

As director of curriculum, I was determined to find a writing program that served the needs of all of our students. I wanted a program that combined the best modern practices with the principles of classical education as defined by such disparate educators as the Roman rhetorician Quintilian and nineteenth-century British reformer Charlotte Mason. I felt strongly that students could be confident, persuasive writers by the eighth grade if they received the right combination of models and practice. Above all, I wanted to avoid the wasted years that led to faltering communication in college and beyond.

I examined quite a few programs. Each in its own way seemed to be lacking—both the modern courses and those purporting to be classically inspired. Nothing seemed to be "just right." Some programs were difficult to use. Others seemed too frivolous on the one hand or too heavy on the other. Still others lacked the necessary incremental steps.

The book you have in your hand is the fruit of my dissatisfaction. This is a curriculum built on the solid foundations of the past and framed with the vitality of the present. This is a curriculum that has been tested by ancient, medieval, and modern kids, and proven reliable for the ages. Along with caring teachers and a diet of good books, the Writing & Rhetoric series has taken the young people of The Oaks, kids from all sorts of advantaged and disadvantaged backgrounds, and shaped them into fine communicators. As a current eighth-grade teacher, I am often delighted by the rhetorical firepower in my classroom.

Imitation as a Foundation for Learning Writing

An examination of the theory and practice of modern composition reveals some obvious problems. Too often students are asked to brainstorm, "prewrite," or "freewrite" according to their personal interests. This means, in essence, that they are supposed to conjure ideas out of thin air. When faced with a blank piece of paper, many students naturally draw a blank. They lack a conversation in their heads about where to begin. Good writing requires content. It abhors a vacuum.

Students are also expected to write with no clear model before them. Modern composition scolds traditional writing instruction as rote and unimaginative. It takes imitation to task for a lack of freedom and personal expression. And yet effective communication from writer to reader always requires some sort of form and structure. Many of history's greatest writers learned by imitation. Benjamin Franklin, for example, taught himself to write by studying classic books and copying whole passages verbatim. He would then put the book aside and try to reconstruct the passage from memory.

Today's emphasis on originality and creativity has failed. When students lack a form by which to express their ideas, their creativity lacks vitality. As Alexander Pope tells us in his "An Essay on Criticism": "True Ease in Writing comes from Art, not Chance, / As those move easiest who have learn'd to dance." In other words, writing takes the same kind of determined study as ballet or diving. Creativity uses conventional form as a stage or a springboard from which to launch grand jetés and somersaults.

But there's yet another problem. Too often students are expected to tackle complex writing assignments without learning the necessary intermediate steps. Without due concern, teachers require summer vacation narratives, persuasive letters, research papers, and poetic descriptions. All of these forms require skills that must be developed in stages. The assumption is that because most everyone can speak English well enough to be understood, and form letters with a pencil, that everyone should be able to write well. And yet how many of us would expect a child to sit at a piano, without piano lessons, and play a concerto? How many of us would expect a child with a hammer and a chisel and a block of marble to carve the statue of David as well as Michelangelo?

Writing is never automatic. The skills of the trade will not miraculously materialize somewhere along the school way. They take years to master. This is because writing demands thoughtfulness, organization, grammatical skill, rhetorical skill, and an ear for the English language. Most children have a natural inclination for one or two of these skills. Rarely do they have a knack for all. The other skills need to be developed and matured.

When it comes down to it, writing is simply thinking on paper. Or thinking in some digital realm. Writing is thought translated to symbols—the symbolic language of the alphabet. The difficulty lies in the process of translation. I may picture a face or a waterfall clearly in my mind. It's quite another thing to describe the face or waterfall articulately in writing. I may have beautiful arguments on the tip of my tongue for buying a Great Dane puppy, but can I make the case persuasively on a piece of paper? The thinking comes first; the writing comes second. Both need to mature together.

What Is to Be Done

If we have lost our way, it rarely helps to plunge blindly forward. It often helps to retrace our steps. And so it is with writing. We have much to learn from the wisdom of the ages. The Greeks developed a system of persuasive speaking known as rhetoric. The Romans, who came later, were also in love with rhetoric, but they took it to the next level. In order to prepare their young students for dazzling oration, the Romans invented a complementary system of persuasive writing.

This writing system was so dynamic, so effective, that it outlasted the Roman Empire, the Middle Ages, and the Renaissance. It even survived into early modern times. This method employed fluent reading, careful listening, models for imitation, and progressive steps. In short, it did many of the things that are out of fashion today, but gave us writers like Cicero and John Milton.

The Romans in the Greek-speaking part of the Empire called their system the *progymnasmata* (pro-gym-naz-ma-ta). This strange, mouthful of a word derives from the same root for exercise as do "gymnasium" and "gymnastics." It means "preliminary exercises." The goal of these lessons is to prepare students for rhetoric, which is the art of writing well and speaking persuasively. This method assumes that students learn best by reading excellent examples of literature and by growing their skills through imitation. Successful writers study great writing. Successful orators study great speeches.

Each exercise is intended to impart a skill (or tool) that can be employed in all kinds of writing and speaking. The exercises are arranged from simple to more complex. What's more, the exercises are cumulative, meaning that later exercises incorporate the skills acquired in preceding exercises. This means, for example, that the skill of reporting or narrating (derived from the narrative exercise) will be regularly practiced and used in future exercises. While engaging in praising an individual (encomium exercise), a student will need to report or narrate an important event or achievement. While comparing two individuals (comparison exercise), a student will often need to praise an individual (encomium).

Studying and acquiring the skills imparted by the *progymnasmata* (hereafter abbreviated *progym*) exercises is much like the way in which we acquire skill in cooking or in a sport like soccer. In the case of cooking, students must first learn the foundational skills of measuring, pouring, and mixing. Then they must learn skills relating to using a frying pan and oven. Each recipe requires the employment of these foundational skills—no matter how complicated it is. A sport like soccer also requires the mastery of basic skills such as kicking, passing, and dribbling. These foundational skills are carried forward into every soccer play and every game strategy.

Think of the *progym* as a step-by-step apprenticeship in the art of writing and rhetoric. What is an apprentice? It is a young person who is learning a skill from a master teacher. Our students will serve as apprentices to the great writers and great stories of history.

Quintilian, one of the master teachers of Rome, tells us that good habits are the foundation of education. In his *Institutio Oratoria*, he writes, "Once a bad habit has become ingrained, it is easier to break than bend. So strong is custom formed in early years." This master teacher also tells us that natural ability is nothing if it is not "cultivated by skillful teaching, persistent study, and continuous and extensive practice in writing, reading, and speaking."

Getting Started

The place to begin is reading, which should be encouraged as one of life's great pleasures from a child's earliest days. Parents should introduce books to babies as soon as they can keep their eyes open. Babies love to hear the sound of their parents' voices. They love the feeling of snuggling in a parent's lap. They love bright books and pictures. Reading helps develop joint attention, which is necessary for any language acquisition. The more a child reads and is read to, the better the foundation for writing. And if a parent feels he or she has been negligent in reading, it's never too late to get started.

The necessary corollary is that we must limit screens: TV, the Internet, and video games should stay off as much as possible! Without realizing it, many parents sabotage the ability of their children to think by allowing an excess of these media. Researchers are telling us, in no uncertain terms, that an imbalance of electronics can be harmful to clear thinking and focused attention. If children don't have time for books, they don't have time for glowing screens. (Unless, of course, that glowing screen contains a book.) Even boredom and daydreaming can be more productive than too much media exposure! A brain needs rest in order to do the hard work of synthesizing information, problem solving, and making connections between ideas.

Next to reading, it's important for children to get comfortable with the formation of letters. Children should work on penmanship to strengthen neural pathways that allow thinking and writing at the same time. Once writing mechanics come easily, it is much easier to make progress in the complex skill of "thinking on paper." As is often the case, there's more to a fine motor skill than meets the eye. With writing, children must learn to grip the pencil properly, to move their arms and wrists smoothly, and to stay focused on the page. Keep practice sessions short, but frequent—about ten minutes a day for seven- and eight-year-olds.

Before children begin *Writing & Rhetoric: Fable*, they should also know how to identify and create a complete sentence. In other words, they should be able to recognize the presence or absence of a subject or a predicate, and know how to use capital letters and simple punctuation. The sentence is the DNA of written ideas.

Note to Teachers

After researching the historic choices, we have decided to capitalize the names of the animals that act as characters in the fables. Other animals (such as the dog in the newspaper story example given on page 5) are not capitalized in an effort to teach students proper capitalization. Hence, the Lion and the Mouse in the fable in lesson 1 are capitalized because they are characters in the story who are named by their animal name. That is not true of the dog, which is the subject of a newspaper story. We have attempted to consistently represent this throughout the book. You may want to explain the difference in usage to your students.

After This—Formal Rhetoric

The formal study of rhetoric will develop in students a solid theoretical understanding of rhetoric, helping them to better understand why and how to employ the skills they have acquired while studying these exercises. The *progym* will prepare your students to enjoy transforming that blank sheet of paper into a spectacular view from atop the pinnacle of their own imagination.

Best Foot Forward

The *Progym* and the Practice of Modern Writing

Although the *progym* are an ancient method of approaching writing, they are extraordinarily relevant today. This is because modern composition owes almost everything to the *progym*. Modern writing borrows heavily from many of the *progym*'s various exercises. For example, modern stories are essentially unchanged from the ancient fable and narrative forms. Modern expository essays contain elements from the ancient *chreia*, the refutation/confirmation, and other *progym* exercises. Persuasive essays of today are basically the same as the ancient commonplace and thesis exercises. In this series, you can expect your students to grow in all forms of modern composition—narrative, expository, descriptive, and persuasive—while at the same time developing unique rhetorical muscle.

The *progym* cover a host of the new Common Core Standards for English and the Language Arts. In the *Fable* book these include:

- Asking and answering questions to demonstrate understanding of the text
- Recounting stories and fables from diverse cultures
- Describing characters in a story
- Determining the meaning of words and phrases in the text
- Distinguishing one's point of view from the point of view of story characters
- Explaining how an illustration enhances the text
- Providing reasons to support an opinion
- Writing narratives to develop imagined experiences

While the goals of the Common Core Standards are certainly worthwhile, the *progym* derive their strength from the incremental and thorough development of each form of writing. The Writing & Rhetoric series does not skip from form to form and leave the others behind, but rather builds a solid foundation of mastery by blending the forms. For example, no expository essay can truly be effective without description. No persuasive essay can be convincing without narrative. All good narrative writing requires description and all good persuasive writing requires expository elements. Not only do the *progym* demand strong organization, but they retain all of the power of classical rhetoric.

Here is how the progym develop each stage of modern composition:

1. Fable—Narrative

2. Narrative—Narrative with descriptive elements

3. *Chreia* & Proverb—Expository essay with narrative, descriptive, and persuasive elements

4. Refutation & Confirmation—Persuasive essay with narrative, descriptive, and expository elements

5. Commonplace—Persuasive essay with narrative, descriptive, and expository elements

6. Encomium & Vituperation—Persuasive essay with narrative, descriptive, and expository elements

7. Comparison—Comparative essay with narrative, descriptive, and expository elements

8. Description & Impersonation—Descriptive essays with narrative, expository, persuasive, and comparative elements

9. Thesis Part 1—Persuasive essay with narrative, descriptive, expository, and comparative elements

10. Thesis Part 2—Persuasive speech with narrative, descriptive, expository, and comparative elements, as well as the three rhetorical appeals

11. Declamation—Persuasive essay or speech that marshals all the elements of the *progym* and brings them to bear upon judicial matters

As you can see, the *progym* move quickly to establish the importance of one form to another.

Objectives for *Fable*

Here are some of the major objectives for the exercises found in this book:

1. Expose students to the form of fables as well as culturally important examples.

2. Model fluent reading for students and give them practice reading short texts.

3. Give students practice copying texts accurately.

4. Strengthen working memory through dictation, thus improving storage and manipulation of information.

5. Increase understanding of the flexibility and copiousness of language through sentence manipulation.

6. Facilitate student interaction with well-written texts through question and answer and through exercises in summary and amplification.

7. Give students opportunities to creatively imitate sentences and whole fables.

8. Introduce the concepts of main idea and character traits.

Lesson 1

Fabulous Fables

Life has many hard lessons to teach us, doesn't it? A boy who has the habit of telling lies will not be believed, even when he is telling the truth. A girl who bosses her friends around will quickly find herself without any friends at all. A man who boasts about his amazing strength might bump into a much stronger person. A woman who spends more money than she earns will soon find herself with empty pockets. These lessons can be very painful to learn if they actually happen to us. But if we learn our lessons from a clever story, we can avoid some of the pain that comes with growing wiser. A **fable**[1] is just such a story. Its purpose is to save us from painful mistakes.

A fable is a short story that teaches a **moral** lesson. These stories help us learn the difference between right and wrong. But fables are not just lectures such as "don't tell lies" or "don't be stubborn." A fable illustrates the lesson with the foolishness of people and animals. If no one believes the shepherd boy when wolves attack his sheep, we can easily see the danger of lying. If the donkey breaks his neck by insisting

---

1. All of the bolded words in this book (other than category titles) are in the glossary at the back of the book.

1

on jumping off the cliff, we can see the danger of stubbornness. Isn't it much more enjoyable to hear a story than to have someone lecture us? That way, we can see a fool in action and not feel so foolish ourselves.

At the end of every fable, we are likely to find a moral. The moral tells us exactly what we need to learn from the fable. Consider the moral a word of friendly advice. Most morals are actually **proverbs**, which are wise sayings that can help us be wiser for the rest of our lives if we live by them.

We can hardly mention the word "fable" without thinking of Aesop. Although we know almost nothing for certain about his life, we do know that Aesop was the greatest of the fable tellers. He is said to have lived sometime in the sixth century before Christ, born a slave in the region of Phrygia in Asia Minor. This same region plays host to the legends of King Midas (of the golden touch) and the city of Gordium, where Alexander the Great is said to have cut through the Gordian Knot. From Phrygia, Aesop was supposedly sold to a master on the island of Samos, where he proved to be so clever that he eventually won his freedom. Ancient historians tell us that he was killed in the city of Delphi. Like Homer 200 years before him, Aesop probably never wrote down his stories. His fables were passed along from storyteller to storyteller and other stories that he never told were credited to him. His fame kept growing, even after he was dead.

The following is one of Aesop's most famous tales. Listen carefully because it will be read only once. Afterwards, you will be asked to tell it back to your teacher, a classmate, or a recording device.

The Lion and the Mouse

A Lion lay asleep in the shady forest, his great head resting on his paws. A timid little Mouse came upon him unexpectedly, and in her fright and haste to get away, she ran across the Lion's nose. Roused from his nap, the Lion laid his huge paw angrily on the tiny creature to kill her.

"Spare me!" begged the poor Mouse. "Please let me go and someday I will surely repay you."

The Lion was much amused to think that a Mouse could ever help him. He laughed so hard that the whole ground shook. But as he was a generous Lion, he let the poor creature go.

Some days later, while stalking his prey in the forest, the Lion was caught in the toils of a hunter's net. Unable to free himself, he filled the forest with his angry roaring. The Mouse knew the voice and quickly found the Lion struggling in the net. Running to one of the great ropes that bound him, she gnawed it until it parted, and soon the Lion was free.

"You laughed when I said I would repay you," said the Mouse. "Now you see that even a Mouse can help a Lion."

Tell It Back—Narration

- <u>Narration</u> is telling a story. Tell back the fable of *The Lion and the Mouse* as best as you remember it using your own words. This is a fabulous way to store up the fable in your mind like a precious treasure. It also helps you grow better at organizing your thoughts and at expressing yourself in writing. For further practice, you can record your telling back into your favorite recording device and listen to it afterwards.

- Try to keep the events of the story in their proper order. What happens first? What happens second? And so on.

Here's the first sentence to help you get started:

A Lion lay asleep in the shady forest, his great head resting on his paws.

Talk About It—Rhetoric Today

1. The word "fabulous" comes from the Latin word *fabula*, which means "fable." Today we most often mean something excellent or wonderful when we say "fabulous." For instance: "Wow! Those are fabulous sneakers!" But the original meaning was more like "hard to believe." What are some reasons why a fable is fabulous or "hard to believe"?

2. What do you think would be a good lesson—a good moral—to take away from the fable *The Lion and the Mouse*?

3. <u>The Golden Rule</u> also seems like a fitting moral for this fable. Do you know the Golden Rule?

   "In everything, do to others what you would have them do to you."

   Why would the Golden Rule be a good moral for this fable?

4. Have you ever been strong and helped someone who was weak? Have you ever been helped by someone who was stronger than you?

5. Recently in the news, a dog rescued his owner from drowning in the Colorado River. The owner fell out of her raft and found herself trapped underneath it in the swirling, rushing water. The dog dived under the raft and freed his owner from the ropes and, grabbing her hair in his mouth, pulled her to safety. What are the similarities of this news report to *The Lion and the Mouse*? What are the differences?

Go Deeper—

<u>Always use complete sentences when filling in the blank spaces.</u>

1. Circle the <u>one sentence</u> in the fable *The Lion and the Mouse* that captures its main idea.

2. Which proverb would best serve as a moral lesson of the fable? Circle the letter:
   a. "Rude parents make rude children."—Chinese proverb
   b. "Only real friends will tell you when your face is dirty."—Italian proverb
   c. "When a mighty tree falls, the goats eat its leaves."—African proverb
   d. "Even the strong sometimes need the friendship of the weak."

3. The word "**timid**" comes from the Latin word *timidus*, which means "fearful." Because the Mouse is described by the **adjective** "timid," what might be another word to describe her?

   a. brave   b. troublesome
   c. excited   d. shy

   Write a complete sentence that describes how a timid boy might act when he walks into his new classroom on the first day of school. The meaning of the word should be clear by the way you use it in your sentence.[2]

   _____

   _____

4. Circle the adjective that best describes the Lion. Why did you pick this word?
   fierce   lazy   wise   sleepy   honest

   _____

   _____

5. At the end of this fable, do you think the Lion changes or does he stay the same? Give a reason for your answer.

   changes   stays the same

   _____

   _____

   _____

2. For this and any other exercise, if you run out of space, use a separate sheet of paper.

Writing Time

1. **COPYWORK**—In the space provided, neatly copy the following sentence:

   The Lion laughed so hard that the whole ground shook.

   _____

   _____

2. **DICTATION**—Your teacher will read to you about lions. Please listen care-fully! After your teacher reads the statement once, she will read it slowly again and include the punctuation marks. Your task will be to write down the sentences as your teacher reads them one by one.

   _____

   _____

   _____

   _____

   _____

   _____

   _____

   _____

   _____

   _____

   _____

_____

_____

_____

3. **SENTENCE PLAY**—"The Lion laughed so hard that the whole ground shook." Can you think what else might happen if you heard a Lion laughing? Maybe the Lion laughed so hard that monkeys fell from the trees. Maybe the Lion laughed so hard that it sounded like thunder. Think of two ways to finish the following sentences:

● The Lion laughed so hard that _____

_____.

● The Lion laughed so hard that _____

_____.

4. **REWRITE** the fable using a Mouse in the role of the strong animal. What sort of weak animal would you need to make the story work? How would the trap be different?

Examples: An Ant saves a Mouse from a snapping trap.

A Spider saves a Mouse that has fallen into a jar of honey.

 # The Lion and the Mouse

A Lion lay asleep in the shady forest, his great head resting on his paws. A timid little Mouse came upon him unexpectedly, and in her fright and haste to get away, she ran across the Lion's nose. Roused from his nap, the Lion laid his huge paw angrily on the tiny creature to kill her.

"Spare me!" begged the poor Mouse. "Please let me go and someday I will surely repay you."

The Lion was much amused to think that a Mouse could ever help him. He laughed so hard that the whole ground shook. But as he was a generous Lion, he let the poor creature go.

Some days later, while stalking his prey in the forest, the Lion was caught in the toils of a hunter's net. Unable to free himself, he filled the forest with his angry roaring. The Mouse knew the voice and quickly found the Lion struggling in the net. Running to one of the great ropes that bound him, she gnawed it until it parted, and soon the Lion was free.

"You laughed when I said I would repay you," said the Mouse. "Now you see that even a Mouse can help a Lion."

The Mouse and the _____

_____

_____

_____

_____

_____

_____

_____

_____

_____

_____

_____

_____

_____

_____

_____

_____

_____

● Why do you suppose changing a famous story can be a helpful way to learn how to tell your own stories?

_____

_____

_____

Speak It

After you finish writing, read your fable to a classmate and listen to his fable. How are your fables different and how are they similar? Tell your classmate one thing you like about the way he changed the story.

Another way to practice speaking is to record yourself on a tablet computer or other recording device. Read the original fable back-to-back with your fable. Which fable is longer? Which fable has more action? Which fable best fits the moral?

Lesson 2

The Master Storyteller

"Once upon a time..."

Those are four magical words, aren't they? When we hear them, we know we're about to be carried off to a fabulous make-believe land.

The science-fiction movie series *Star Wars* begins just like a fairy tale: "A long time ago, in a galaxy far, far away . . ." People love a good story, whether they lived hundreds of years ago or will live hundreds of years from now. Yes, people love a good story. Everyone. Everywhere.

Whether you live in Los Angeles or New York, Timbuktu or Kathmandu, or the town of Gnaw Bone, Indiana, as long as you are a human being you will love stories.

Why do we all love stories so well? Maybe it's because each of our lives is a story. Each of us has a beginning, a middle, and an end. We also play a part in a bigger story—the story of our family, the story of our school, the story of our country, the story of our religious faith. We long to understand our part in those bigger stories.

More than anything, we love stories because we want to see how people solve their problems. It's inspiring to see how Ludwig van Beethoven wrote beautiful music even though he was deaf, or how Ray Charles played jazz piano even though he was blind, or how Bethany Hamilton returned to surfing even after a shark bit off her arm. We love to see how detectives solve mysteries or how weak athletes overcome stronger athletes to win a competition.

One of the important goals of this series of writing exercises is to help you become a better storyteller. By studying a master storyteller like Aesop, you can learn to write fables, too. "But why?" you might ask. "Why is it important for me to tell fables and stories well? Why must I work so hard at my writing?"

▶ Well, can you think of any good reasons?

_____

_____

_____

Since people love stories, it only makes sense that you will be listened to by others, and you will be heard better, if you can tell stories. Of course, you already tell stories—jokes and tattles and daily happenings—but I mean telling stories in a zesty, exciting way so that other people really, really enjoy listening to you.

▶ Pastors, priests, and rabbis tell stories in their sermons.
▶ Presidents tell stories in their speeches.
▶ Scientists tell stories in their science books.
▶ Teachers tell stories in their lessons.
▶ Camp counselors tell stories around the campfire.
▶ Parents tell stories at bedtime.

Have you ever wondered why so much storytelling is going on? It's because people want to share something important with you and they know you'll listen best when you hear a story. It only makes sense that if you want to be listened to, you will also learn to tell stories.

Every master storyteller is like a master chef. She has a spice chest filled with spices to help her flavor her story soup. In this chest, she has the zest of **vocabulary**—all the wild, sparkly, crackling, popping words she can think of. The more vocabulary she pours into her story soup, the tastier her story will be.

A master storyteller can also change how words are ordered in a sentence. For example, she could write the sentence this way:

- Out of the window, Goldilocks jumped.

Or she could write it this way:

- Goldilocks jumped out of the window.

By changing the order of words, the storyteller keeps her audience hungry for more.

Two of the most important spices in the story chest are **amplification**, which is to make a story longer, and **summary**, which is to make a story shorter. A master storyteller must be able to draw out or shrink a story to suit the needs of her audience.

When there's plenty of time, a storyteller may amplify or stretch out the story to make it more exciting: "And then the Wolf, with his fangs bared and spit dripping from his lips, approached the house made of straw. Even the tiniest breath of a breeze caused that house to tremble and sway. The Wolf scratched the door—scritch, scritch, scritch—and in a gravelly, growly voice said, 'Let me in, Little Pig!'"

When there isn't much time or space, a storyteller may simply say: "And then the Wolf approached the house of straw. He said, 'Let me in, Little Pig!'"

Let's take a look at a fable told two ways, first as an amplification, and then as a summary.

Three Young Bulls and a Lion

ALion was watching three young Bulls feeding in an open field. He tried to attack them several times, but they kept together and helped each other to drive him off. The Lion had little hope of eating them because he was no match for three strong Bulls with their sharp horns and hoofs. But he could not keep away from that field, for it is hard to resist watching a good meal, even when there is little chance of getting it.

Then one day the young Bulls quarreled over which one of them should eat a patch of sweet clover. They pawed the ground angrily, butted each other, and scratched each other with their horns. When the hungry Lion came to look at them and lick his chops, he found them in separate corners of the field, as far away from one another as they could get.

It was now an easy matter for the Lion to attack them one at a time. He ate all three young Bulls with the greatest satisfaction and **relish**.

MORAL: *In unity is strength.*

Now let's look at the same fable, written as a summary.

Three Young Bulls and a Lion

A Lion tried to attack three Bulls, but they kept together and helped each other to drive him off. The Lion waited and watched for a chance to eat the Bulls. One day the young Bulls quarreled. When the hungry Lion came to look at them, he found them far apart. It was now easy for the Lion to eat them one at a time.

▶ Does the fable still make sense in summary form? Is the summary useful in some way? Which version do you like best, the summary (short form) or amplification (long form)? Why?

_____

_____

_____

You will have an opportunity to amplify and summarize the fables and stories in this book. By changing the length of the fables, you will see more clearly how stories are put together. More than likely, you've already taken something apart: a flashlight, a Lego creation, etc. The process of taking something apart and putting it back together again helps you to understand how it works. Your ability to write stories will improve as you take apart stories and put them back together again.

Tell It Back—Narration

Without looking at the fable, tell the longer version of *Three Young Bulls and a Lion* as best as you remember it using your own words. For further practice, you can record your telling back into your favorite recording device and play it afterwards.
- Keep the events of the story in their proper order.
- Use a sprinkling of words from the fable, such as the word "relish."

Here's the first sentence to help you get started:

A Lion was watching three young Bulls feeding in an open field.

Talk About It—

1. "Unity is strength" is the motto of the nation of Bolivia. What does this saying mean? In Latin, another way to express this idea is *unus pro omnibus, omnes pro uno*, which means "One for all, all for one." Why were the young Bulls in this fable so foolish? How did ignoring *unus pro omnibus, omnes pro uno* lead to their destruction?

2. Think about the Lion watching the young Bulls from a distance. According to Aesop, "It is hard to resist watching a good meal, even when there is little chance of getting it." Can you think of an instance when you wanted something badly, but your parents did not let you have it? What was it that your parents wouldn't let you have? Why did your parents not want you to have the thing you craved? What lesson did you learn?

Go Deeper—

Always use complete sentences when filling in the blank spaces.

1. Which proverb from around the world would best serve as a moral lesson for the fable *Three Young Bulls and a Lion*? Circle the correct answer:
   a. "A mad bull should not be tied up with a thread."—Spain
   b. "Do not steal prey from a hungry lion."—Italy
   c. "United we stand, divided we fall."—United States (Kentucky)
   d. "Water can float a boat, but it can sink it, too."—China

2. Which verse from the Hebrew Scriptures would best serve as a moral lesson for the fable *Three Young Bulls and a Lion*? Circle the correct answer:

   a. "Though one may be overpowered,/ two can defend themselves./ A cord of three strands is not quickly broken."—Ecclesiastes 4:12

   b. "Lips that speak knowledge are a rare jewel."—Proverbs 20:15

   c. "If a man's bull injures the bull of another and it dies, they are to sell the live one and divide both the money and the dead animal equally." —Exodus 21:35

   d. "There is nothing new under the sun."—Ecclesiastes 1:9

3. Relish is not only the chopped pickles you put on your hot dogs. Since the hungry Lion eats the Bulls "with the greatest satisfaction and relish," the word "relish" probably means:

   a. disgust

   b. pleasure

   c. sadness

   d. wickedness

4. How is the personality of the Lion in the second fable (*Three Young Bulls and a Lion*) different than the Lion from the first fable (*The Lion and the Mouse*)? How are they similar? Explain your answer.

   _____

   _____

   _____

   _____

   _____

   _____

   _____

_____

_____

_____

Writing Time

1. **COPYWORK**—In the space provided, neatly copy the following sentence: The Lion had little hope of eating them because he was no match for three strong Bulls.

   _____

   _____

   _____

   _____

2. **DICTATION**—Your teacher will read either a short poem or information about bulls. Please listen carefully! After your teacher reads once, he will read slowly again and include the punctuation marks. Your task will be to write down the sentences as your teacher reads them one by one.

   _____

   _____

   _____

   _____

   _____

3. **SENTENCE PLAY**—"When the hungry Lion came to look at the Bulls, <u>he licked his chops</u>."

To lick its chops, an animal licks the sides of its jaws with its very long tongue. Can you lick your chops?

Think of two ways to show that the Lion is very hungry when he arrives at the field.

● When the hungry Lion came to look at the Bulls,

_____

_____.

● When the hungry Lion came to look at the Bulls,

_____

_____.

4. **SUMMARY**—When you summarize a story, you want to keep it short. Keep only the most important ideas. The rest of the writing can be done away with.

a. Read *Three Young Bulls and a Lion* again. While you're reading it, keep your eye out for the main idea. The main idea is the most important idea in a fable or story. Things happen (actions) in each fable that help us to see the main idea clearly. Search the fable to find the most important action. The moral of the story is the main idea of the fable but it shows up first as part of the action (what happens) of the story. Once you have decided what the main idea of the story is, circle or highlight it. This sentence will help you to write your summary.

b. Underline any words that are necessary to telling the story. Use these words to tell the story briefly in your summary.

c. Cross out any words or sentences that are extra details. These details might make the fable more fun to read, but they aren't necessary for readers to understand the main idea.

d. Rewrite the fable in four sentences or less.

Lesson 2: The Master Storyteller

Three Young Bulls and a Lion

ALion was watching three young Bulls feeding in an open field. He tried to attack them several times, but they kept together and helped each other to drive him off. The Lion had little hope of eating them because he was no match for three strong Bulls with their sharp horns and hoofs. But he could not keep away from that field, for it is hard to resist watching a good meal, even when there is little chance of getting it.

Then one day the young Bulls quarreled over which one of them should eat a patch of sweet clover. They pawed the ground angrily, butted each other, and scratched each other with their horns. When the hungry Lion came to look at them and lick his chops, he found them in separate corners of the field, as far away from one another as they could get.

It was now an easy matter for the Lion to attack them one at a time. He ate all three young Bulls with the greatest satisfaction and relish.

MORAL: *In unity is strength.*

SUMMARY:

_____

_____

_____

_____

_____

_____

_____

_____

_____

5. **AMPLIFICATION**—Below is the summary of an Indian fable called *The Hunter and the Doves*, which also teaches "unity is strength." Make the summary of this story longer.

a. You can add description and details. What do the Doves look like? How does the King Dove look different from the others? What does the Hunter look like? Where are the Doves coming from and where are they going? What types of seeds are scattered on the ground and what do they taste like to the birds? Does the King Dove or the Hunter have a name?

b. You can expand the moral lesson by telling why "unity is strength" and why it is important to be unified.

The Hunter and the Doves

An Indian Fable

A flock of Doves spotted some seeds scattered on the ground. When they flew down to eat the seeds, a Hunter hiding in the tree above dropped a net upon them. The birds were trapped! Keeping his head, the King Dove told the other Doves to each lift up a string of the net and flap her wings. By doing so, the Doves were able to lift the net together and carry it off as they escaped through the air.

MORAL: *In unity is strength.*

_____

_____

_____

_____

_____

_____

_____

_____

_____

_____

_____

_____

Speak It—

Read your amplification of *The Hunter and the Doves* to your class or your teacher. Listen to other amplifications. Pick an amplification you like and explain why. (Note to solo students: you may record your amplification on a tablet computer or other recording device and listen to it afterwards.)

What are some of the things you did to make the story longer?

_____

_____

_____

_____

_____

_____

_____

_____

Lesson 3 ·······································

Anthropomorphism— Rabbits in Jackets, Brainy Crows

Do you know the story of Peter Rabbit? Poor Peter, a young rabbit, loses his jacket and shoes in Mr. McGregor's garden, and Peter Rabbit is almost caught and baked in a meat pie. Peter escapes to his home, where he is sent to bed while his sisters enjoy blackberries and milk. Now, there's something strange about this story. First of all, rabbits don't wear jackets and shoes. They don't sleep in beds either. *The Tale of Peter Rabbit* is an example of a story with anthropomorphism. Peter acts like a naughty human boy.

Anthropomorphism (an-thro-po-mor-phism) is a long word that means something really very simple. *Anthropos* in Greek means "man" while <u>morph</u> means "to change form." So put them together and the word roughly means "a human changing form." Whenever a storybook animal acts like a human being, that's anthropomorphism. Whenever an animal talks, or wears clothes, or smokes a pipe, or eats with a fork, that's anthropomorphism.

We see anthropomorphism in famous characters such as the March Hare from *Alice's Adventures in Wonderland*, who wears a pocket watch and goes to crazy tea parties. The flying monkeys from *The Wizard of Oz* wear caps and vests, and they follow a wicked king of the monkeys. By contrast, Aslan the lion from *The Lion, the Witch and the Wardrobe* is a wise king of the beasts who sits on a throne and battles against evil. Other famous anthropomorphisms are Winnie the Pooh, Puss in Boots, The Three Bears, and the Wolf in *Little Red Riding Hood*.

▶ Why do you suppose so many writers use anthropomorphism in their stories? Is there any advantage to using an animal character instead of a human?

_____

_____

_____

_____

The following is a fable about a Crow with a very serious problem. How does Aesop use anthropomorphism to make the story more interesting?

The Crow and the Pitcher

The weather was burning hot, and the birds could find nothing to drink. Even the creek beds carried only sand. A thirsty Crow found a pitcher with a little water in the bottom. But the pitcher was tall and had a narrow neck, and no matter how hard she tried, the Crow could not reach the water. "Oh, I will surely die of thirst!" the poor bird groaned. In despair, she came up with an idea. She gathered a pile of small pebbles and then, one by one, she dropped them into the pitcher. As each pebble plunked to the bottom, the water rose a little higher. Soon the water was high enough for the Crow to dip her beak into it. How sweet and cool it tasted! By using her wits, the Crow had saved her life.

Tell It Back—Narration

Without looking at the fable, tell back *The Crow and the Pitcher* as best as you remember it using your own words. For further practice, you can record your telling back into a device and listen to it afterwards.

Lesson 3: Anthropomorphism—Rabbits in Jackets, Brainy Crows

- Keep the events of the story in their proper order.
- Use a sprinkling of words from the fable, such as the word "thirst."

Here's the first sentence to get you started:

The weather was burning hot, and the birds could find nothing to drink.

Talk About It—

1. Remember that anthropomorphism is an animal acting like a person. What does the Crow do that seems human? Why is anthropomorphism important to this fable, *The Crow and the Pitcher*? How would the story be different if the main character possessed human hands?

2. Writers anthropomorphize animals to stand for certain types of people. For instance, a cat can stand for a lazy person. A pig can stand for a sloppy person. What type of animal would best stand for these types of people?

   a. Thief

   b. Violent bully

   c. Liar

   d. Coward

   e. Wise man or woman

   f. Weight lifter

   g. Trickster

3. Look carefully at the illustration of Jemima Puddle-Duck by Beatrix Potter and a painting of a duck by Hiroshige. In which of these pictures is the bird anthropomorphized? Explain your answer.

Go Deeper—

1. Circle the one sentence in *The Crow and the Pitcher* that captures the main idea of the fable.

2. Which sentence would best serve as a moral lesson of the fable? Circle the correct answer:
   a. "Better to go hungry than thirsty."
   b. "If you're in trouble, use your brain."
   c. "Crows are smart birds."
   d. "When you need help, use pebbles."

3. What season is described in this story? Give a reason for your answer.

   _____

   _____

4. Write down three phrases from the fable that provide clues that the weather is dangerously dry?

   a. _____

   b. _____

   c. _____

5. Circle the adjective that best describes the Crow. Why did you pick this word?
   silly   rude   clever   brave   stubborn

   _____

   _____

   _____

Writing Time—

1. **COPYWORK**—In the space provided, neatly copy the following sentence:

   As each pebble plunked to the bottom, the water rose a little higher.

   _____

   _____

   _____

2. **DICTATION**—Your teacher will read to you about crows. Please listen carefully! After your teacher reads once, he will read slowly again and include the punctuation marks. Your task will be to write down the sentences as your teacher reads them one by one.

   _____

   _____

   _____

   _____

   _____

   _____

   _____

   _____

3. **SENTENCE PLAY**—"<u>Even the creek beds carried only sand.</u>" Using this sentence as a model, write another sentence to show the seriousness of the dry spell.

You could start your sentence with:

    Even the fountains . . .

    Even the ponds . . .

    Even the birdbaths . . .

_____

_____

4. **COPIOUSNESS**—Welcome to your first exercise in writing copiously. This means that you are going to work on finding different ways to say the same thing. The word "copious" comes from the Latin word *copious*, meaning "plentiful or abundant." If you were to say, "My neighbor talks copiously," you probably mean that your neighbor uses lots of words and is a bit of a blabbermouth. If you were to say, "I found copious amounts of candy in the jar," you mean that you've hit the jackpot—lots and lots of candy.

Whether you know it or not, you speak copiously all the time. Take the typical kid who has ice cream on the brain. She may say, "Wow, it's hot. What about ice cream?" "I'm boiling. Ice cream sure sounds amazing." "I feel like I'm stuck in a furnace. I need ice cream." "I'm a puddle of sweat. I'll perish without ice cream." And so on. **Copiousness** comes naturally, especially when you want something really, really badly.

For starters, we're going to work on changing our **nouns** and adjectives.

A noun is a person, place, thing, or idea. An adjective adds description to a noun and helps us to "see" it more clearly. For example, when you sell cold lemonade, "lemonade" is a noun because it is a thing. The word "cold" is an adjective because it describes the lemonade. Another example: When you visit your sweet old grandmother, "grandmother" is a noun because it is a person. What are the adjectives that describe grandmother? There are two.

_____ _____

Mark the nouns and adjective in the sentence below. Place an *N* over the nouns and an *ADJ* over the adjective.

She gathered a pile of small pebbles.

Hint: There are three nouns, but only one of them is described by an adjective.

Replace the adjective "small" in this sentence with different adjectives that have close to the same meaning. See if you can come up with three.

a. She gathered a pile of _____ pebbles.

b. She gathered a pile of _____ pebbles.

c. She gathered a pile of _____ pebbles.

5. **AMPLIFICATION**—The fable *The Crow and the Pitcher* is shortened below. Read it over and think of ways you can make it longer.

a. You can add description, names, and details. What does the Crow look like? What signs does she see that the weather is very hot? How does she feel besides thirsty? Does she feel dizzy, sweaty, or weak?

b. You can expand the moral lesson by telling why using your brain is important.

The Crow and the Pitcher

A Crow was dying of thirst during a terrible drought. She found a pitcher with water at the bottom, but the neck was too narrow for her to reach it. Dropping pebbles into the pitcher, the Crow raised the level of water and saved her life.

Lesson 3: Anthropomorphism—Rabbits in Jackets, Brainy Crows

6. **SUMMARY**—When you summarize a story, you want to keep only the most important ideas. The rest of the writing can be done away with.

a. Read the fable *The Hare and the Partridge* below. While you're reading it, keep your eye out for the main idea. The main idea is the most important idea in a fable or story. Things happen in each fable that help us to see the main idea clearly. Search the fable to find the most important action. The moral of the story is the main idea of the fable but it shows up first as part of the action of the story. Once you have decided what the main idea of the story is, circle or highlight it. This sentence will help you to write your summary.

b. Underline any words that are essential to telling the story. Use these words to tell the story briefly in your summary.

c. Cross out any words or sentences that are extra details. These details might make the fable more fun to read, but they aren't necessary for readers to understand the main idea.

d. Rewrite the following fable in four sentences or less.

The Hare and the Partridge

by Jean de La Fontaine

A Hare and a Partridge lived side by side in a big field. They were good neighbors and got along well enough. One day, a pack of Hunting Dogs came tearing across their field, barking and snapping and attacking everything that moved. The Hare was forced to run for cover through the trees. She found a place to hide under a pile of sticks and crouched there, shivering and quaking. Sadly, her overheated body gave off a smell that drew the Dogs' noses. In a jiffy, the Dogs found the poor Hare and scattered her pile of sticks. Then they finished her off.

Later, after the Dogs had left, the Partridge stepped out of hiding. She stuck her beak in the air and scoffed to the dead Hare, "You always said you were so swift. So now what has become of your feet? I'd much rather be a Partridge than a Hare any day."

At that moment, out of the clear, blue sky, a Hawk struck the Partridge with her sharp talons and carried her off to her nest.

MORAL: *Never laugh at another person's misfortunes.*

_____

_____

_____

_____

_____

_____

_____

_____

_____

_____

Speak It—

Read your summary of *The Hare and the Partridge* to your class or teacher. Or record your summary on a recording device, and listen to it afterwards.

What are some other ways you could have shortened the fable?

Lesson 4 ···

Summary—
Sour Grapes

Have you ever met anyone who was **"sour grapes"**? See if you can guess the meaning of this expression by the way it's used in these sentences:

- Veronica didn't win first prize in the piano contest, so she said the trophy was ugly, but that was just sour grapes.

- Don't behave with an attitude of sour grapes because you weren't invited to the birthday party.

- The loss of the football game caused the fans to have sour grapes about the event.

This expression comes to us from Aesop's famous fable *The Fox and the Grapes*. After you read the fable, try to come up with your own definition of "sour grapes."

The Fox and the Grapes

A Fox one day spied a beautiful bunch of ripe grapes hanging from a vine twisting around the branches of a tree. The grapes seemed ready to burst with juice, and the Fox's mouth watered as he gazed longingly at them. "That's just what I need to quench my thirst," he thought.

The bunch hung from a **lofty** branch, and the Fox had to jump for it. The first time he jumped, he missed it by a long way. "I'll have to do better than that," said he. "Those are probably the sweetest, most delicious grapes in all of Greece." So he walked off a short distance and took a running leap at the bunch, only to fall short once more. Again and again he tried, but in vain.

"What a fool I am," he said. "Here I am wearing myself out to get a bunch of grapes that are probably sour anyway. I wouldn't bother to eat them if they were an inch off the ground." Away he walked very, very scornfully.

MORAL: *Many people despise what is beyond their reach.*

Lesson 4: *Summary—Sour Grapes*

Tell It Back—Narration

Without looking at the fable, tell back *The Fox and the Grapes* as best as you remember it using your own words. For further practice, you can record your telling back on device and play it afterwards.

- Keep the events of the story in their proper order.
- Use a sprinkling of words from the fable or moral, such as the word "despise."

Here's the first sentence to get you started:

A Fox one day spied a beautiful bunch of ripe grapes hanging from a vine twisting around the branches of a tree.

Talk About It—

1. What is your definition of the idea of "sour grapes"? Use the expression "sour grapes" in a complete sentence.

2. Of the following three sentences, two are examples of "sour grapes," and one is not. Identify each, labeling them as either "sour grapes" or "not sour grapes," and try to remember a time when you or someone else you know acted like "sour grapes." Tell the story to your classmates or record it on your favorite device and listen afterwards.

   Mary said, "I'm glad I wasn't invited to Lucy's party. Her mother makes awful cupcakes." _____

   Bobby said, "I can play baseball better than you can!" _____

   "That's not a very good prize," said Jason after he lost the contest.

   _____

3. Look carefully at this illustration of *The Fox and the Grapes*. Is the fox gazing longingly at the grapes, or does it have the attitude of sour grapes?

Go Deeper—

1. Because the Fox hopes to quench his thirst with juicy grapes, the word <u>quench</u> probably means:

   a. satisfy

   b. increase

   c. jump

   d. starve

2. Because the Fox has to jump for a lofty branch, the word "lofty" probably means:

   a. low

   b. large

   c. sour

   d. high

   Use the word "lofty" in your own complete sentence.

   _____

   _____

3. Did you notice the word **despise** in the moral? "Many people despise what is beyond their reach." The Latin root for "despise" is *despicio*. The word *de* means "down" and *spicio* means "I look." Can you guess what despise means? Look up the word "despise" in a <u>dictionary</u>. Write the definition in the space below.

   Definition _____

   _____

   _____

Sometimes when we feel bad because we can't have something we want, we say things to put it down and make ourselves feel better about not having it. The Fox despised the grapes he couldn't have by saying they must be sour.

Once there was a boy whose parents would not allow him to see a movie he wanted to see. Write a "sour grapes" statement that he might say to despise the movie.

Sentence _____

_____

4. "Many people despise what is beyond their reach." What might be another way to write this moral? Circle the correct answer.

   a. "Don't jump for things out of reach."
   b. "It's easy to dislike what you can't have."
   c. "Foxes are intelligent creatures."
   d. "High grapes always taste sour."

5. Circle the adjective that best describes the Fox at the beginning of the fable.

   crazy   thirsty   intelligent   stupid   sly

6. Circle the adjective that best describes the Fox at the end of the fable. Below, explain why you picked this word.

   mean   lazy   clever   irritated   happy

   _____

   _____

   _____

   _____

Writing Time—

1. **COPYWORK**—In the space provided, neatly copy the following sentence:

   The bunch hung from a lofty branch, and the Fox had to jump for it.

   _____

   _____

   _____

   _____

2. **DICTATION**—Your teacher will read to you about foxes. Please listen carefully! After your teacher reads once, she will read slowly again and include the punctuation marks. Your task will be to write down the sentences as your teacher reads them one by one.

   _____

   _____

   _____

   _____

   _____

   _____

   _____

   _____

3. **SENTENCE PLAY**—"<u>Those are probably the sweetest, most delicious grapes</u> <u>in all of Greece.</u>" Using this sentence as a model, write another sentence to show what the Fox would say if he found lemons in Lebanon.

"Those are probably the _____

_____."

Now what would the Fox say if he found soda pop in Singapore?

"That is probably the _____

_____."

What would the Fox say if he found roses in Rwanda?

"Those are probably the _____

_____."

4. **COPIOUSNESS**—Remember that there are often lots of ways to say the same thing. Learning to write copiously will help you to stretch for new, richer words.

Mark the nouns and adjectives in the sentence below. Place an *N* over the nouns and an *ADJ* over the adjective. A noun is a person, place, thing, or idea. An adjective describes a noun.

A Fox one day spied a beautiful bunch of grapes.

a. Replace the adjective "beautiful" with a different adjective that has close to the same meaning. Replace any nouns that are left blank in the sentences below with nouns of your choosing.

1) A Fox one day spied a _____ bunch of grapes.
(adjective like beautiful)

2) A Fox one day spied a _____ bunch of grapes.
(adjective like beautiful)

3) A Fox one day spied a beautiful bunch of _____.
(noun)

4) A Fox one _____ spied a beautiful
(noun—time-of-day word)

_____ of _____.
(noun)   (noun)

5) A _____ one _____
(noun—animal)   (noun—time-of-day word)

spied a _____ bunch of _____.
(any adjective)   (any noun)

b. Take another look at the moral of this fable. Rewrite this sentence by changing as many words as you can, especially the key words "despise" and "reach."
The new sentence should mean nearly the same thing as the old sentence.

"Many people despise what is beyond their reach."

_____

_____

5. **SUMMARY**—Read the fable *The Fox and the Grapes* again. Cross out any unnecessary sentences. Search the fable to find the most important action. The
moral of the story is the main idea of the fable but it shows up first as part of
the action of the story. Once you have decided what the main idea of the story
is, circle or highlight it. Underline the sentences that support it. You may also
rewrite sentences to make them shorter.

The Fox and the Grapes

A Fox one day spied a beautiful bunch of ripe grapes hanging from a vine
twisting around the branches of a tree. The grapes seemed ready to burst

with juice, and the Fox's mouth watered as he gazed longingly at them. "That's just what I need to quench my thirst," he thought.

The bunch hung from a lofty branch, and the Fox had to jump for it. The first time he jumped, he missed it by a long way. "I'll have to do better than that," said he. "Those are probably the sweetest, most delicious grapes in all of Greece." So he walked off a short distance and took a running leap at the bunch, only to fall short once more. Again and again he tried, but in vain.

"What a fool I am," he said. "Here I am wearing myself out to get a bunch of grapes that are probably sour anyway. I wouldn't bother to eat them if they were an inch off the ground." Away he walked very, very scornfully.

MORAL: *Many people despise what is beyond their reach.*

Hint: See if you can do away with five or six sentences.

SUMMARY—

_____

_____

_____

_____

_____

_____

_____

_____

_____

_____

_____

6. **REWRITE** the fable *The Fox and the Grapes* using a different animal and a different fruit or unattainable object. For example, you could write about a Dog who wants a plate of fried chicken on the table. Or you could write about a Cat that wants to catch a Frog at the bottom of a pond. Keep the same moral lesson, which is "Many people despise what is beyond their reach."

_____

_____

_____

_____

_____

_____

_____

_____

_____

_____

_____

_____

_____

_____

_____

_____

_____

_____

Speak It—

Learning something by heart is called memorization. Memorization is an important part of speaking. It is important because it will help you to learn organization, increase your vocabulary, and give you ideas for creating new sentences. Believe it or not, memorization is much easier for young people than it is for older people. You're at the perfect age to become an expert memorizer.

Memorize *The Fox and the Grapes* word for word and recite it to your class. Here are some strategies you can use to help your memorization:

1. Give the fable your full attention. Read it carefully without any distractions.

2. Break the fable down into three sections: beginning, middle, and end.

Here is the <u>beginning</u>, where we meet both the Fox and the grapes:

A Fox one day spied a beautiful bunch of ripe grapes hanging from a vine twisting around the branches of a tree. The grapes seemed ready to burst with juice, and the Fox's mouth watered as he gazed longingly at them. "That's just what I need to quench my thirst," he thought.

Here is the <u>middle</u>, where the Fox attempts to reach the grapes:

The bunch hung from a lofty branch, and the Fox had to jump for it. The first time he jumped, he missed it by a long way. "I'll have to do better than that," said he. "Those are probably the sweetest, most delicious grapes in all of Greece." So he walked off a short distance and took a running leap at the bunch, only to fall short once more. Again and again he tried, but in vain.

Here is the <u>end</u>, where the Fox decides to walk away:

"What a fool I am," he said. "Here I am wearing myself out to get a bunch of grapes that are probably sour anyway. I wouldn't bother to eat them if they were an inch off the ground." Away he walked very, very scornfully.

MORAL: *Many people despise what is beyond their reach.*

Memorize each section in order. Master one section before moving on to the next. You may make your own recording and play it back to help you memorize, or listen to ours. Repetition helps with memorization.

3. Some students find it helpful to sing the words they want to memorize. Other students like to write the words over and over again. In any case, it is important to speak the words out loud and to ask your parents or siblings to listen to you recite.

A Note on Proper Elocution

Whether you are reciting a poem or reading a story out loud, you want to speak in such a way that the audience can hear you "loud and clear." The art of speaking skillfully is known as elocution. So, what goes into proper elocution?

First of all, you should make sure you are pronouncing all of your words clearly. This means you are making each word sharp and crisp instead of blending them together and mumbling. You want to say, "Betty eats butter better on bread," with each word separate from the next. You don't want to say, "Bettyeatsbutterbetteronbread."

Secondly, good posture is very important for speaking loudly enough. You can't breathe very well if you are slouched over. Stand up straight and tall, square your shoulders, and look at your audience. Look directly into their eyes. This will help your listeners know that you are a confident speaker. They will enjoy your recitation more when they see how confident you are.

Finally, don't speak too quickly. It's hard to understand a recitation that blasts off like a rocket ship. You will want to speak at a good pace and pause every now and then to let your words sink in.

You will delight to your listeners if you can stand up straight, look into their eyes, and speak loud and clear at just the right pace.

These instructions appear at the back of this text as well and are relevant for each "Speak It" section in the book. Please consult it as regularly as you need to.

Lesson 5

Amplification—
The Road to Disaster

Whether deserved or not, donkeys (also known as asses) have a bad reputation. Kenyans say that a donkey rewards kindness with a kick. Italians say that the back of an ass is used to beatings. The Dutch say that if you give an ass oats, he'll try to eat thorns and thistles instead.

> G.K. Chesterton wrote a poem called "The Donkey" and describes him thus:
> With monstrous head and sickening cry
> And ears like errant wings,
> The devil's walking parody
> On all four-footed things.

The words "ass" and "fool" have come to mean the same thing. To be called an ass is to be called a fool. Like so many of our words, the word "fool" made its way into English from Latin. The Roman *follis* was a leather bag used to heat the fire in a blacksmith's shop. So, a fool has a *follis* for a head. In other words, he's an airhead or a windbag. This next fable by Aesop clearly illustrates the danger of being a fool.

47

The Ass and His Driver

An Ass was being driven along a road leading down the mountainside, and the animal suddenly took it in his silly head to choose his own path. He could see his barn at the foot of the mountain. To him, the quickest way down seemed to be over the edge of the nearest cliff. Just as he was about to leap over, his Master caught him by the tail and tried to pull him back.

"Stop!" cried the Master. "Stop or you will surely break your neck!"

The stubborn Ass would not yield and pulled with all his might.

"Very well," said his Master, "go your way, you **willful** beast, and see where it leads you."

With that he let go, and the foolish Ass tumbled head over heels down the mountainside.

MORAL: *Listen to good advice and avoid the road to* ***disaster***.

Tell It Back—Narration

Without looking at the fable, tell back *The Ass and His Driver* as best as you remember it using your own words. For further practice, record your telling back on a device and play it afterwards.

● Keep the events of the story in their proper order.

● Use a sprinkling of words from the fable, such as the word "willful."

Here's the first sentence to get you started:

An Ass was being driven along a road leading down the mountainside, and the animal suddenly took it in his silly head to choose his own path.

Talk About It—

1. Foolishness comes in many shapes and sizes, and the Ass is foolish in more than one way. In what ways is the Ass foolish?

2. No doubt you have heard of a child's disobedience leading to disaster. Every year, kids who play with matches cause house and apartment fires. Thousands of kids injure themselves, too, by ignoring parents' warnings about fireworks. The Hebrew Scriptures contain some advice for parents. One proverb says, "Train a child in the way he should go, and when he is old, he will not turn from it" (Proverbs 22:6). Suppose the Ass is a child. Should a parent, like the Master, let a willful child go his own way and see where it leads him? Is that a good parent? Why or why not?

3. Martin Luther King Jr. braved tear gas, jail, and death threats to help bring an end to segregation in America. Jessica Watson braved high winds, high waves, and days of loneliness to become the youngest person (age sixteen) to sail alone around the world. Edmund Hillary and Tenzing Norgay braved blizzards, avalanches, and deadly cracks in the ice to climb Mount Everest, the highest mountain in the world. Sometimes it's not a bad thing to be

willful and persevering! Can you think of anyone else in literature or history for whom a certain stubbornness was a good and necessary quality?

Go Deeper—

1. Because the Ass insists on doing as he pleases, the word "willful" probably means:
   a. complaining
   b. stubborn
   c. wise
   d. crabby

2. Look up the word "disaster" in a dictionary. Write the definition in the space below and then use it in your own complete sentence.

   Definition _____

   _____

   _____

   Sentence _____

   _____

   _____

3. Here are some other morals for the fable *The Ass and His Driver*. Which moral would NOT work? Circle the correct answer.
   a. "Some people will not listen to reason."
   b. "Always take a shortcut if you can."
   c. "A fool gets what he deserves."
   d. "A willful beast will go his own way."

4. Circle the adjectives that best describe the Ass at the beginning of the fable.

   stubborn & foolish   quick & strong   brave & wise

5. Circle the adjectives that best describe the Ass at the end of the fable.

quick & strong   stubborn & foolish   brave & wise

6. Does the Ass change his ways in this fable or does he remain the same? Give a reason for your answer.

changes   remains the same

_____

_____

Writing Time—

1. **COPYWORK**—In the space provided, neatly copy the following sentence:

   Just as he was about to leap over, his Master caught him by the tail and tried to pull him back.

   _____

   _____

   _____

2. **DICTATION**—Your teacher will read to you about donkeys. Please listen carefully! After your teacher reads once, she will read slowly again and include the punctuation marks. Your task will be to write down the sentences as your teacher reads them one by one.

   _____

   _____

   _____

   _____

   _____

_____

_____

_____

3. **SENTENCE PLAY**—"<u>Stop or you will surely break your neck!</u>" What other warnings could the Master have yelled at the Ass? Write two sentences below.

a. "Stop or . . . _____

b. _____

c. Some sentences are very simple. Here is an example:

The Ass tumbled.

Only three words! Most sentences are a little more complicated. They contain words that help us to picture the sentence more clearly. This sentence, for instance, tells us what kind of Ass it is, how the Ass tumbled, and where it tumbled.

The foolish Ass tumbled head over heels down the mountainside. Do you see that we have amplified the sentence for the same reason we amplify stories? We amplify stories to give more detail and to make the pictures more clear in our heads. In a similar way, we also amplify sentences to give more detail. Yet we can still have a complete sentence if all the picture words are subtracted by crossing them out.

The ~~foolish~~ Ass tumbled ~~head over heels down the mountainside~~.

Now we're back to the basic sentence:

The Ass tumbled.

1) In the following sentences, cross out the picture words to form basic sentences of three words each. Then write the three-word sentences on the blanks provided.

Example: A ~~red~~ robin hopped ~~quickly across the lawn~~.
Changed to: A robin hopped.

- The willful elephant stood stiffly in the middle of the street.

    _____

- A scared squirrel climbed quickly to a very lofty branch.

    _____

- The white snow flew wildly through the trees.

    _____

- The bare swords flashed red in the setting sun.

    _____

2) Look again at this sentence:

    The Ass tumbled.

Although this sentence is correct and complete, it is not clear where the Ass tumbled. Did he tumble in the road? Did he tumble down a waterfall? How did the Ass tumble? Did he tumble gracefully? Did he tumble softly? What kind of Ass tumbled? Was he a purple Ass? Was he a gentle Ass?

The foolish Ass tumbled head over heels down the mountainside.

From this sentence, we know that the Ass was a foolish beast. We know that he tumbled head over heels. We know that he tumbled down the mountainside.

Expand the sentences below to give your readers a more clear and interesting picture.

Example: The clown slipped.
Changed to: The crazy clown slipped carelessly on a banana peel.

- The dog ran.

  _____

  _____

- The girl laughed.

  _____

  _____

- The snake crawled.

  _____

  _____

4. **COPIOUSNESS**—Mark the nouns and adjectives in the sentence below. Place an *N* over the nouns and an *ADJ* over the adjectives. Remember that a noun is a person, place, thing, or idea. An adjective describes a noun.

   The Ass suddenly took it in his silly head to choose his own path.

   a. Let's drop the adjective "silly" from the sentence. Replace the word "silly" with other adjectives that mean nearly the same thing. Use a thesaurus only if you get stuck.

      1) The Ass suddenly took it in his _____
         head to choose his own path.   (adjective for silly)

      2) The Ass suddenly took it in his _____
         head to choose his own path.   (adjective for silly)

3) The Ass suddenly took it in his _____
(adjective for silly)
head to choose his own path.

b. Now let's take the same sentence and change the nouns without changing the meaning of the sentence.

The <u>Ass</u> suddenly took it in his silly <u>head</u> to choose his own <u>path</u>.

_____

_____

_____

c. Rewrite the moral by replacing as many words as you can, but keep the same meaning.

<u>Listen</u> to <u>good</u> advice and <u>avoid</u> the <u>road</u> to <u>disaster</u>.

_____

_____

5. **AMPLIFICATION**—The fable *The Ass and His Driver* is shortened below. Read it over and think of ways you can make it longer.

a. You can add description, names, and details. What does the Ass look like? What about the mountains and the Master? What does the Ass do?

b. You can amplify the moral lesson by telling why disobedience can lead to disaster.

The Ass and His Driver

An Ass wanted to take the shortest path home by going over a mountain cliff. His Master tried to stop him and grabbed his tail, but at last he was forced to let go. The stubborn beast fell to his death.

MORAL: *Listen to good advice and avoid the road to disaster.*

_____

_____

_____

_____

_____

_____

_____

_____

_____

_____

_____

_____

_____

_____

_____

- After you finish writing, compare your amplification with a classmate's or family member's. What are some other ways you could have amplified your fable?

Speak It—

The following is a poem about a foolish, willful child whose life ends in disaster. Just as you did with *The Fox and the Grapes*, divide the poem into smaller parts and memorize each part before moving to the next. Also, consider recording it or using our recording of this story to aid your memorization.[1]

The Story of Augustus, Who Would Not Have Any Soup

by Heinrich Hoffman

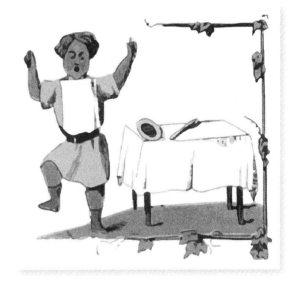

Augustus was a chubby lad;
Fat ruddy cheeks Augustus had:
And everybody saw with joy
The plump and hearty, healthy boy.
He ate and drank as he was told,
And never let his soup get cold.
But one day, one cold winter's day,
He screamed out, "Take the soup away!
O take the nasty soup away!
I won't have any soup today."

Next day, now look, the picture shows
How lank and lean Augustus grows!
Yet, though he feels so weak and ill,
The naughty fellow cries out still
"Not any soup for me, I say:
O take the nasty soup away!
I won't have any soup today."

---

1. To review the elocution instructions, see page 152.

The third day comes: Oh what a sin!

To make himself so pale and thin.

Yet, when the soup is put on table,

He screams, as loud as he is able,

"Not any soup for me, I say:

O take the nasty soup away!

I WON'T have any soup today."

Look at him, now the fourth day's come!

He scarcely weighs a sugar-plum;

He's like a little bit of thread,

And, on the fifth day, he was—dead!

Lesson 6

Summary: Belling the Cat

Cats and mice have long been enemies. People tamed wildcats in the first place to protect their stores of grain from hordes of hungry mice. Cats are the perfect mouse hunters.

There are many delightful proverbs about cats and mice from around the world. The Senegalese say that when a mouse makes fun of a cat, a hole must be nearby. The French say that a mouse with only one hole is soon caught. And the Chinese say that a careless mouse, chewing on a cat's tail, should beware of sudden death!

Aesop is responsible for giving us the expression "to bell the cat." See if you can guess what it means "to bell the cat" by the way it is used in these sentences:

- It would be great to deal with that bully, but who is willing to bell the cat?
- Mrs. Spike is such a mean lady, I wish we could hear her coming. Anyone want to bell the cat?
- It would be easier to bell the cat than sneak one of Grandma's cookies.

The Mice in Council

Something had to be done about the Cat! Hardly a day went by that the Mice didn't hear of some brother or sister, aunt or uncle, having gotten gobbled down by the Cat. The Mice lived in such constant **dread** of her claws that they hardly dared to stir from their dens by night or day. Finally, they called a meeting to decide on a plan to free themselves from their fearsome enemy.

Many plans were discussed, but none of them sounded good enough. At last, a very Young Mouse got up and said, "I have a plan that seems very simple, but I know it will be successful. All we have to do is to hang a bell about the Cat's neck. When we hear the bell ringing, we will know immediately that our enemy is coming."

All the Mice were much surprised that they had not thought of such a plan before. "Hurrah for the Young Mouse!" they shouted.

As they were cheering and rejoicing over their good fortune, an Old Mouse stood up. Shaking a finger at the gathering, he said, "I will say that the plan of the Young Mouse is very good. But let me ask one question: Who will bell the Cat?"

Lesson 6: Summary: Belling the Cat

Tell It Back—Narration

Without looking at the fable, tell back *The Mice in Council* as best as you can remember it using your own words. For further practice, you can record it on your recording device of choice and play it back afterwards.

- Keep the events of the story in their proper order.
- Use a sprinkling of words from the fable, such as the word "dread."

Here's the first sentence to get you started:

Something had to be done about the Cat!

Talk About It—

1. What is your definition of "belling the cat"? Use the expression "belling the cat" in a complete sentence.

2. Recently, a group of fishermen in Canada returned to their cabin on a lake, only to find that a bear had broken in and eaten some of their food. Pancake mix lay on the floor and the refrigerator stood open, but the bear was nowhere to be seen. The fishermen started making their dinner. As they were eating in the dining room, they heard the same bear pushing on the front door. They talked quickly about what to do. Together they pushed the table against the door. The bear pushed back, but the fishermen were able to hold the door closed. One man had a good idea—"Let's go outside and throw a pot of hot water in its face." It may have been a good idea, but no one wanted to face the bear outside in the dark. How is this story similar to and different from the fable *The Mice in Council*?

3. No man in the Hebrew Scriptures was as strong and dangerous as Samson. He tore apart a lion with his bare hands and slew many of his enemies with no weapon other than the jawbone of an ass. His enemies wanted to learn the secret to his terrible strength and capture him. So they paid money to a pretty woman, Delilah, and urged her to discover his secrets. After much

pleading and pestering, Samson told Delilah that the secret to his strength was his long, unruly hair. Well, as soon as Samson fell asleep that night, Delilah cut his hair off. Samson's enemies jumped out of hiding and grabbed him. Because his hair was cut, Samson's strength was gone and he could no longer fight. His enemies tied him up and dragged him away. How is this story similar to and different from the fable *The Mice in Council*?

4. The Cheshire Cat found in the storybook *Alice's Adventures in Wonderland* is one of the most famous portraits of a cat. If you were a mouse, would you trust this cat? Why or why not?

Go Deeper—

1. Circle the best moral for the fable *The Mice in Council*:
   a. "Cats are wicked pets."
   b. "Kindness is important."
   c. "Some things are easier said than done."
   d. "It is better to make friends rather than enemies."

2. Because the Mice lived in constant dread and hardly ever stirred from their dens, the word "constant" probably means:
   a. steady
   b. rare
   c. happy
   d. growing

3. Look up the word "dread" in a dictionary, then write the definition in the space below. Next, use it in your own complete sentence about a child afraid of a monster under his bed.

   Definition _____

   _____

Sentence _____

_____

4. The Mice and the Cat are the perfect animals for this fable because the Mice are fearful creatures and the Cat is fearsome. Which of the following pairs of creatures would work equally well, one fearful and the other fearsome?

    a. frogs and a turtle

    b. worms and a bird

    c. lions and a wolf

    d. monkeys and an ape

Writing Time—

1. **COPYWORK**—In the space provided, neatly copy the following sentence: As they were cheering and rejoicing over their good fortune, an Old Mouse stood up.

_____

_____

_____

2. **DICTATION**—Your teacher will read to you about cats. Please listen carefully! After your teacher reads once, she will read slowly again and include the punctuation marks. Your task will be to write down the sentences as your teacher reads them one by one.

_____

_____

_____

_____

_____

_____

_____

3. **SENTENCE PLAY**

a. "<u>All we have to do is hang a bell about the Cat's neck</u>." Using this sentence as a model, write another sentence to show what the Young Mouse would say if he wanted to tie something noisy to part of a rat. For example: "All we have to do is tie a tin can to the Rat's tail."

"All we have to do is _____

_____

_____."

b. What would the Young Mouse say if he wanted to put something sticky on part of a human?

"All we have to do is _____

_____

_____."

c. What would the Young Mouse say if he wanted to put something shiny on a part of an owl?

"All we have to do is _____

_____

_____."

d. <u>Something had to be done about the Cat</u>! This is a strong first sentence because it grabs the reader's attention. Think of two other sentences to begin the fable.

• _____

_____

• _____

_____

4. **COPIOUSNESS**—Mark the nouns and adjectives in the following sentence. Place an *N* over the nouns and an *ADJ* over the adjective. Remember that a noun is a person, place, thing, or idea. An adjective describes a noun. (This sentence contains an interesting noun called a possessive noun. A possessive noun owns something and uses an *'s*. Can you find it?)

The Mice lived in constant fear of the Cat's claws.

a. Let's add an adjective to the sentence by describing the Cat's claws. Remember that the Mice lived in fear of these claws, so you should describe them as something scary.

Example: The Mice lived in constant fear of the Cat's fierce claws.

   1) The Mice lived in constant fear of the Cat's _____ claws.

   2) The Mice lived in constant fear of the Cat's _____ claws.

   3) The Mice lived in constant fear of the Cat's _____ claws.

b. Now let's take the same sentence and change as many words as we can without changing the meaning of the sentence. Let's call the Mice rodents. Do Cats have different names as well?

The <u>Mice</u> lived in <u>constant</u> <u>fear</u> of the <u>Cat's</u> <u>claws</u>.

_____

_____

c. Just for fun, let's rearrange and rewrite the sentences below with different **subjects**. (A subject is what the sentence is about.) How would you rewrite the sentences to keep the same meaning?

Sample sentence: The bright moon was howled at by the Dog.
New subject: The Dog howled at the bright moon.

1) The Cat's claws were feared by the Mice.

The Mice _____.

2) The Cat gobbled down the Mice.

The Mice _____

3) A meeting was called by the Mice to decide on a plan.

The Mice _____.

5. **SUMMARY**—Read the fable *The Mice in Council* again. Read it once more and cross out any unnecessary sentences. Keep only the main idea and the sentences that support it. You may also rewrite sentences to make them shorter.

The Mice in Council

Something had to be done about the Cat! Hardly a day went by that the Mice didn't hear of some brother or sister, aunt or uncle, having gotten gobbled down by the Cat. The Mice lived in such constant dread of her claws that they hardly dared to stir from their dens by night or day. Finally, they called a meeting to decide on a plan to free themselves from their fearsome enemy.

Many plans were discussed, but none of them sounded good enough. At last, a very Young Mouse got up and said, "I have a plan that seems very simple, but I know it will be successful. All we have to do is to hang a bell about the Cat's neck. When we hear the bell ringing, we will know immediately that our enemy is coming."

All the Mice were much surprised that they had not thought of such a plan before. "Hurrah for the Young Mouse!" they shouted.

As they were cheering and rejoicing over their good fortune, an Old Mouse stood up. Shaking a finger at the gathering, he said, "I will say that the plan of the Young Mouse is very good. But let me ask one question: Who will bell the Cat?"

<u>Hint</u>: See if you can do away with five or six sentences.

SUMMARY—

_____

_____

_____

_____

_____

_____

_____

_____

_____

_____

_____

_____

_____

_____

_____

_____

6. **REWRITE** the fable *The Mice in Council* using different animals. One animal should be a killer like the Cat and the other animals should be food for this animal like the Mice. For example, the killer animal could be a Hawk and the food animals could be Rabbits. Or the killer animal could be a Shark and the food animals could be Seals. Keep the same moral lesson, which is "Some things are easier said than done."

_____

_____

_____

_____

_____

_____

_____

_____

_____

_____

_____

_____

_____

_____

_____

_____

_____

_____

_____

_____

_____

_____

_____

_____

Speak It—

After you finish writing, read your fable to a classmate and listen to her fable.

How are your fables different and how are they similar?

Or read your fable into your favorite recording device, and then play it back.

How else could you have changed it?

Lesson 7

Amplification—
Grasping at Shadows

Advertisers love to make their products sound great by calling them extreme. Extreme taste! Extreme crunch! Extreme adventure! Extreme underarm smell protection! The word "extreme" comes from the Latin word *extremus*, which means "outermost" and "utmost."

But extreme is not always so "terrific." Greed can be defined as "an extreme desire to have something more than a person needs or deserves." Have you ever been in a grocery store or toy store and seen a child throw a greedy fit? At first, the child may ask for something nicely, "Can you buy me a doll, please?" Then the child pesters, "Please, please, please. I only have ten dolls." Next, the child whines or cries, "You never buy me anything. You don't love me!" Finally, the child flings herself on the floor and starts screaming, "I want it, I want it, I waaaaaaaant it!"

The following is a fable by Aesop about a dog that was too greedy.

The Dog and Her Reflection

A Dog had swiped a bone from the butcher's shop, and she was hurrying home with her prize as fast as she could go. As the Dog crossed a narrow footbridge, she happened to look down. She saw herself reflected in the quiet water as if in a mirror. But the greedy Dog did not recognize herself. She thought she saw another Dog carrying a bone much bigger than her own and she felt extremely desirous.

If the Dog had stopped to think she would have known better, but instead she started growling **viciously**. "I want that big bone," she thought. Her fur stood up on the back of her neck and she bared her fangs. The Dog in the river also bared her fangs. In a rage, the Dog dropped her bone and sprang at her reflection, only to find herself swimming for dear life. At last, the Dog managed to reach the shore and scramble out. As she shook the water from her coat, the Dog remembered the lost bone. "Oh, what a stupid Dog I've been!" she cried.

Tell It Back—Narration

Without looking at the fable, tell back *The Dog and Her Reflection* as best as you remember it using your own words. Or you can record it as you remember the story and play it back.

- Keep the events of the story in their proper order.
- Use a sprinkling of words from the fable, such as the word "viciously" (or "vicious").

Here's the first sentence to get you started:

A Dog had swiped a bone from the butcher's shop, and she was hurrying home with her prize as fast as she could go.

Talk About It—

1. People are not usually greedy for bones. What are some things that people can be greedy for?

2. What should parents do when a little one throws a temper tantrum in a store? Should they buy the child what she wants?

3. Have you heard the story *The Golden Touch*? King Midas is a rich ruler, and he already owns a copious amount of gold. And yet Midas loves gold so much that he asks the Greek god Dionysus to give him a magical power—the ability to turn everything he touches into gold. Dionysus grants the wish. At first, Midas is overjoyed. He turns flowers and trees into gold. He turns his clay dishes into plates of gold. But when he wants to eat, Midas is horrified to find that all of his food turns to gold. When he fondly touches his daughter, she turns to gold as well. Then Midas curses his greed and begs Dionysus to take away the magical power. Once again Dionysus grants his wish and the golden touch goes away. How is this story similar to and different from the fable *The Dog and Her Reflection*?

Lesson 7: Amplification— Grasping at Shadows

Go Deeper—

1. What do you think people should learn from the fable *The Dog and Her Reflection*? Write your own moral lesson.

_____

_____

_____

2. Circle the moral that works best for this fable:
   a. "A fool and his money are soon parted."
   b. "Save for a rainy day."
   c. "Falling is easier than rising."
   d. "It is foolish to be greedy."

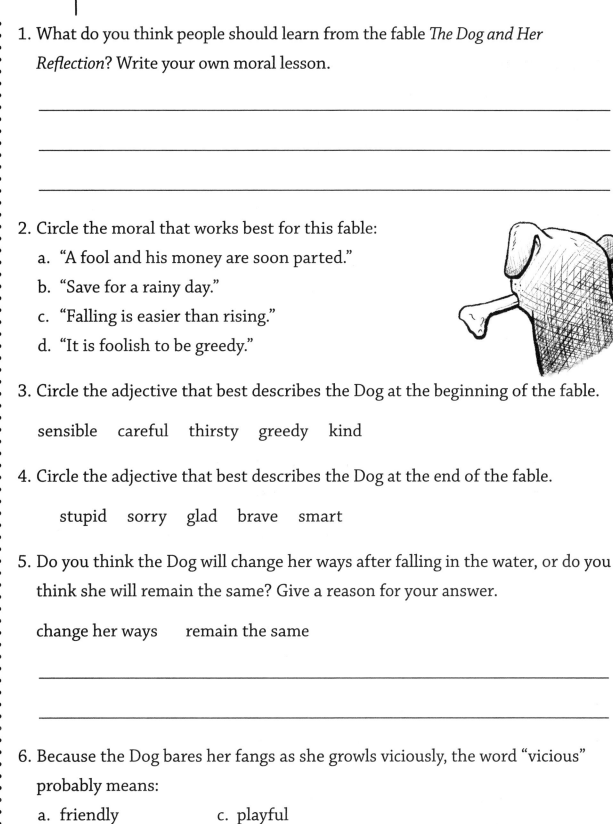

3. Circle the adjective that best describes the Dog at the beginning of the fable.

   sensible   careful   thirsty   greedy   kind

4. Circle the adjective that best describes the Dog at the end of the fable.

   stupid   sorry   glad   brave   smart

5. Do you think the Dog will change her ways after falling in the water, or do you think she will remain the same? Give a reason for your answer.

   change her ways   remain the same

   _____

   _____

6. Because the Dog bares her fangs as she growls viciously, the word "vicious" probably means:
   a. friendly   c. playful
   b. worried   d. fierce

Use the word "vicious" in your own complete sentence.

_____

_____

Writing Time—

1. **COPYWORK**—In the space provided, neatly copy the following sentence:

   As the Dog crossed a narrow footbridge, she happened to look down.

   _____

   _____

   _____

   _____

2. **DICTATION**—Your teacher will read to you about dogs and bones. Please listen carefully! After your teacher reads once, he will read slowly again and include the punctuation marks. Your task will be to write down the sentences as your teacher reads them one by one.

   _____

   _____

   _____

   _____

   _____

   _____

   _____

   _____

Lesson 7: Amplification— Grasping at Shadows

3. **SENTENCE PLAY**—The word "as" tells us that one thing is happening at the same time another thing is happening. What two things are happening in this sentence?

As she ran, she sang.

_____

Here is a sentence from our fable using "as": <u>As she shook the water from her coat, the Dog remembered the lost bone.</u> Using this sentence as a model, write other sentences to show two things the Dog is doing at once.

a. As she barked at the moon,

_____.

b. As she sniffed her food dish,

_____.

c. As she

_____.

4. **COPIOUSNESS**—Mark the nouns and adjectives in the sentence below. Place an *N* over the nouns and an *ADJ* over the adjective. Remember that a noun is a person, place, thing, or idea. An adjective describes a noun.

A Dog swiped a bone from a butcher's shop.

a. Add adjectives to the sentence to describe the <u>bone</u> and the <u>shop</u>.
For example: A Dog swiped a <u>pretty</u> bone from a butcher's <u>sunny</u> shop.

1) A Dog swiped a _____ bone from a

butcher's _____ shop.

2) A Dog swiped a _____ bone from a

butcher's _____ shop.

3) A Dog swiped a _____ bone from a

butcher's _____ shop.

b. Take the same sentence and change the underlined words *without changing the meaning of the sentence*.

A <u>Dog</u> <u>swiped</u> a bone from a butcher's <u>shop</u>.

_____

_____

_____

c. This time, take the same sentence and change as many words as you can *while completely changing the meaning of the sentence*. Change the animal, the action, the object, and the place, but keep the same structure.

A Dog swiped a bone from a butcher's shop.

Example: A <u>T-Rex</u> <u>chewed</u> a <u>tire</u> from a <u>farmer's</u> <u>truck</u>.

_____

_____

d. Again, rearrange and rewrite the sentence using a different subject. Keep the original meaning. Do you remember what a subject is?

A bone was swiped from a butcher's shop by a Dog.

Make "a Dog" the subject of your sentence.

A Dog _____

_____

Lesson 7: *Amplification— Grasping at Shadows*

Make "a butcher's shop" the subject of your sentence.

A butcher's shop _____

_____

5. **AMPLIFICATION**—Below, you'll find a shortened version of *The Dog and Her Reflection*. Read it over and think of ways you can make it longer.

a. You can add description and details.

b. You can expand the moral lesson by telling why it's foolish to be greedy.

The Dog and Her Reflection

Crossing a bridge with a stolen bone, a Dog noticed her reflection in the creek below. Greedily she wanted to seize the bone carried by her mirror image. She jumped into the water and lost her prize.

MORAL: *It is foolish to be greedy.*

_____

_____

_____

_____

_____

_____

_____

_____

_____

_____

_____

_____

_____

_____

_____

_____

6. **WRITE** a true fable about a time in your own life when you were greedy. Can you think of a time when you took more than your fair share of food? Was there a time when you ate too much candy? Have you played video games longer than you should have? Choose one incident and tell the story so that the moral, "It is foolish to be greedy," still holds true.

_____

_____

_____

_____

_____

_____

_____

_____

_____

_____

_____

Speak It—

There are many excellent stories about greed. With your classmates, prepare a dramatic reading of this fairy tale, *The Fisherman and His Wife*, from *Fairy Tales by the Brothers Grimm*. Delivery is an important part of speaking well.

1. Practice your parts so that you know them well. The more you practice, the smoother you will read and the better people will listen. Use a recording device, if possible, to hear how you sound.

2. Try to make your voice sound emotional in the right places. When the Wife is angry, her voice should sound angry. When the Fisherman is scared, his voice should sound scared.

Remember the importance of elocution, which is the art of speaking skillfully! As a speaker you will want to stand up straight, look into the eyes of your audience, and speak loud and clear. Make sure you don't speak too quickly, and pause every now and then to let your words sink in. For more advice, look at the elocution instructions located on page 143.

The Fisherman and His Wife

NARRATOR: There was once a fisherman who lived with his wife in a pigsty, close by the seaside. The fisherman used to go out all day long a-fishing; and one day, as he sat on the shore with his rod, looking at the sparkling waves and watching his line, all of a sudden his float was dragged away deep into the water; and in drawing it up, he pulled out a great fish. But the fish said:

FISH: Pray let me live! I am not a real fish; I am an enchanted prince. Put me in the water again, and let me go!

NARRATOR: Said the man:

FISHERMAN: Oh, ho! You need not make so many words about the matter; I will have nothing to do with a fish that can talk. So swim away, sir, as soon as you please!

NARRATOR: Then he put him back into the water, and the fish darted straight down to the bottom, and left a long streak of blood behind him on the wave.

When the fisherman went home to his wife in the pigsty, he told her how he had caught a great fish, and how it had told him it was an enchanted prince, and how, on hearing it speak, he had let it go again. Said his wife:

WIFE: Did not you ask it for anything? We live very wretchedly here, in this nasty dirty pigsty; do go back and tell the fish we want a snug little cottage.

NARRATOR: The fisherman did not much like the business. However, he went to the seashore; and when he came back there, the water looked all yellow and green. And he stood at the water's edge, and said:

FISHERMAN:

> "O man of the sea!
> Hearken to me!
> My wife Ilsabill
> Will have her own will,
> And hath sent me to beg
>   a boon of thee!"

NARRATOR: Then the fish came swimming to him, and said:

FISH: Well, what is her will? What does your wife want?

NARRATOR: Said the fisherman:

FISHERMAN: Ah! She says that when I had caught you, I ought to have asked you for something before I let you go. She does not like living any longer in the pigsty, and wants a snug little cottage.

FISH: Go home, then; she is in the cottage already!

Lesson 7: Amplification— Grasping at Shadows

NARRATOR: So the man went home, and saw his wife standing at the door of a nice trim little cottage. She said:

WIFE: Come in, come in! Is not this much better than the filthy pigsty we had?

NARRATOR: And there was a parlor, and a bedchamber, and a kitchen; and behind the cottage, there was a little garden, planted with all sorts of flowers and fruits; and there was a courtyard behind, full of ducks and chickens. Said the fisherman:

FISHERMAN: Ah! How happily we shall live now!

WIFE: We will try to do so, at least.

NARRATOR: Everything went right for a week or two, and then Dame Ilsabill said:

WIFE: Husband, there is not near room enough for us in this cottage; the courtyard and the garden are a great deal too small; I should like to have a large stone castle to live in. Go to the fish again and tell him to give us a castle.

FISHERMAN: Wife, I don't like to go to him again, for perhaps he will be angry. We ought to be easy with this pretty cottage to live in.

WIFE: Nonsense! He will do it very willingly, I know. Go along and try!

NARRATOR: The fisherman went, but his heart was very heavy; and when he came to the sea, it looked blue and gloomy, though it was very calm; and he went close to the edge of the waves, and said:

FISHERMAN:

> "O man of the sea!
> Hearken to me!
> My wife Ilsabill
> Will have her own will,
> And hath sent me to beg a boon of thee!"

FISH, *slightly irritated*: Well, what does she want now?

FISHERMAN, *dolefully*: Ah! My wife wants to live in a stone castle.

FISH: Go home, then. She is standing at the gate of it already.

NARRATOR: So away went the fisherman, and found his wife standing before the gate of a great castle.

WIFE: See, is not this grand?

NARRATOR: With that, they went into the castle together, and found a great many servants there, and the rooms all richly furnished, and full of golden chairs and tables; and behind the castle was a garden, and around it was a park half a mile long, full of sheep, and goats, and hares, and deer; and in the court-yard were stables and cow-houses. The fisherman said:

FISHERMAN: Well, now we will live cheerful and happy in this beautiful castle for the rest of our lives.

WIFE: Perhaps we may, but let us sleep upon it before we make up our minds to that.

NARRATOR: So they went to bed. The next morning when Dame Ilsabill awoke it was broad daylight. She jogged the fisherman with her elbow, and said:

WIFE: Get up, husband, and bestir yourself, for we must be king of all the land.

FISHERMAN: Wife, wife, why should we wish to be the king? I will not be king.

WIFE: Then I will.

FISHERMAN: But, wife, how can you be king? The fish cannot make you a king!

WIFE: Husband, say no more about it, but go and try! I will be king.

NARRATOR: So the man went away quite sorrowful to think that his wife should want to be king. This time the sea looked a dark gray color, and was overspread with curling waves and the ridges of foam as he cried out:

Lesson 7: Amplification— Grasping at Shadows

FISHERMAN:

> "O man of the sea!
> Hearken to me!
> My wife Ilsabill
> Will have her own will,
> And hath sent me to beg a boon of thee!"

FISH, *angrily*: Well, what would she have now?

FISHERMAN, *woefully*: Alas! My wife wants to be king.

FISH: Go home, she is king already.

NARRATOR: Then the fisherman went home; and as he came close to the palace, he saw a troop of soldiers, and heard the sound of drums and trumpets. And when he went in, he saw his wife sitting on a throne of gold and diamonds, with a golden crown upon her head; and on each side of her stood six fair maidens, each a head taller than the other.

FISHERMAN: Well, wife, are you king?

WIFE, *grandly*: Yes, I am king.

NARRATOR: And when he had looked at her for a long time, he said:

FISHERMAN: Ah, wife! What a fine thing it is to be king! Now we shall never have anything more to wish for as long as we live.

WIFE: I don't know how that may be. Never is a long time. I am king, it is true; but I begin to be tired of that, and I think I should like to be emperor.

FISHERMAN: Alas, wife! Why should you wish to be emperor?

WIFE: Husband, go to the fish! I say I will be emperor.

FISHERMAN: Ah, wife! The fish cannot make an emperor, I am sure, and I should not like to ask him for such a thing.

WIFE: I am king, and you are my slave; so go at once!

NARRATOR: So the fisherman was forced to go; and he muttered as he went along:

FISHERMAN: This will come to no good. It is too much to ask; the fish will be tired at last, and then we shall be sorry for what we have done.

NARRATOR: He soon came to the seashore; and the water was quite black and muddy, and a mighty whirlwind blew over the waves and rolled them about, but he went as near as he could to the water's brink, and said:

FISHERMAN:

> "O man of the sea!
> Hearken to me!
> My wife Ilsabill
> Will have her own will,
> And hath sent me to beg a boon of thee!"

FISH, *furiously*: What would she have now?

FISHERMAN, *scared*: Ah! She wants to be emperor.

FISH: Go home, she is emperor already.

NARRATOR: So he went home again; and as he came near, he saw his wife Ilsabill sitting on a very lofty throne made of solid gold, with a great crown on her head full two yards high; and on each side of her stood her guards and attendants in a row, each one smaller than the other, from the tallest giant down to a little dwarf no bigger than my finger. And before her stood princes, and dukes, and earls: and the fisherman went up to her and said:

FISHERMAN: Wife, are you emperor?

WIFE: Yes, I am emperor.

FISHERMAN: Ah! What a fine thing it is to be emperor!

WIFE: Husband, why should we stop at being emperor? I will be pope next.

FISHERMAN: O wife, wife! How can you be pope? There is but one pope at a time in Christendom.

WIFE: Husband, I will be pope this very day.

FISHERMAN: But, the fish cannot make you pope! Please!

WIFE: What nonsense! If he can make an emperor, he can make a pope. Go and try him. I demand it! I will not be satisfied until I am pope.

NARRATOR: So the fisherman went. But when he came to the shore, the wind was raging and the sea was tossed up and down in boiling waves, and the ships were in trouble, and rolled fearfully upon the tops of the billows. In the middle of the heavens, there was a little piece of blue sky, but toward the south all was red, as if a dreadful storm was rising. At this sight, the fisherman was dreadfully frightened, and he trembled so that his knees knocked together. But still he went down near to the shore, and said:

FISHERMAN:

"O man of the sea!
Hearken to me!
My wife Ilsabill
Will have her own will,
And hath sent me to beg a boon of thee!"

FISH, *booming*: What does she want now?

FISHERMAN, *deathly afraid*: Ah! My wife wants to be pope.

FISH: Go home! She is pope already.

NARRATOR: Then the fisherman went home, and found Ilsabill sitting on a throne that was two miles high. And she had three great crowns on her head, and around her stood all the pomp and power of the Church. And on each side of her were two rows of burning lights, of all sizes, the greatest as large as the highest and biggest tower in the world, and the least no larger than a small rushlight. Looking up at her greatness, the Fisherman said:

Lesson 7: Amplification— Grasping at Shadows

FISHERMAN: Wife, are you pope?

WIFE: Yes, I am pope.

FISHERMAN: Well, wife, it is a grand thing to be pope; and now you must be easy, for you can be nothing greater.

WIFE: I will think about that.

NARRATOR: Then they went to bed. But Dame Ilsabill could not sleep all night for thinking what she should be next. At last, as she was dropping asleep, morning broke, and the sun rose. Looking at the sun through the window, she thought:

WIFE: Ha! After all I cannot prevent the sun rising.

NARRATOR: At this thought, she was very angry, and wakened her husband, and said:

WIFE: Husband, go to the fish and tell him I must be lord of the sun and moon. I will be like God.

NARRATOR: The fisherman was half asleep, but the thought frightened him so much that he started and fell out of bed.

FISHERMAN: Alas, wife! Cannot you be easy with being pope? Please!

WIFE: No, I am very uneasy as long as the sun and moon rise without my leave. Go to the fish at once!

NARRATOR: Then the man went shivering with fear; and as he was going down to the shore, a dreadful storm arose, so that the trees and the very rocks shook. And all the heavens became black with stormy clouds, and the lightnings played, and the thunders rolled; and you might have seen in the sea great black waves, swelling up like mountains with crowns of white foam upon their heads. And the fisherman crept toward the sea, and cried out, as well as he could:

Lesson 7: *Amplification— Grasping at Shadows*

FISHERMAN:

"O man of the sea!

Hearken to me!

My wife Ilsabill

Will have her own will,

And hath sent me to beg a boon of thee!"

FISH, *thundering*: What does she want now?

FISHERMAN, *terrified*: Ah! She wants to be lord of the sun and moon.

FISH: Go home to your pigsty again.

NARRATOR: And the man returned home to his pigsty and found his wife on the dirt floor crying bitter tears. And there they live to this very day.

Lesson 8

Main Idea—
Choosing a Fitting Moral

Even though we don't meet talking animals every day, we certainly bump into people who act like the animals in fables. We meet bullies who act like wolves, beauties who act like peacocks, and stubborn people who act like donkeys.

We often see people driving too fast, zipping past all the cars on the road like a rabbit, only to get stopped by a red light. "Ha! Serves them right," we think. The moral? "Haste makes waste." Or "the fastest drivers reach the stop light first."

And speaking of rude drivers, there's the type that chugs along playing music so loudly that the ground shakes. There they go, slouched behind the wheel, trying to look as cool as a duck in a thunderstorm. When these drivers play their music so loudly, trying so hard to look cool, they're also damaging their hearing and quickly going deaf. What lesson can we draw? "Loud music today, deaf tomorrow."

One great source of material for writing fables is the daily news. You may have heard of any number of silly criminals bungling their crimes. Once there was a bank robber who ran out of a bank with sacks of money in his hands. He jumped into a waiting car and shouted, "Get going! Hurry, before the cops come!" At that point, the robber realized he had accidentally jumped into a police car and was talking to a police officer. Another time, a robber walked into a drugstore and yelled, "This is a robbery!" He pulled a plastic garbage bag over his head to disguise his face, but the only problem was he forgot to cut holes in the bag for his eyes. Blinded by the plastic, he ran into a wall. What moral could you draw from these stories? How about "crime doesn't pay" or "a fool's home is a jail cell"?

The following "fables" are taken from the news. Your task is to match the six morals at the end of this lesson with the six fables presented here. Remember that a moral is a little lesson, a bit of wisdom that you'd like the reader to store away like a squirrel storing nuts.

Here are six morals (or main ideas) to choose from. Write them down in the spaces provided after each fable. Your teacher may ask you to think up other morals to go along with the fables above.

- "Honesty is its own reward."
- "A fool and his money are soon parted."
- "Love your neighbor as yourself."
- "It's easy to be brave from a safe distance."
- "Even the strong sometimes need the help of the weak."
- "Life will humble every person."

1. A Kentucky man and his wife won $27 million in the state lottery. The couple spent their money wildly: gambling at casinos, buying houses and cars, throwing parties, and taking private jet rides. It took only three years for them to lose their fortune and they ended up poor once again.

   Moral:

   _____

   _____

2. The bullfighter strutted bravely into the arena in Mexico City, bowing to the ladies and to the gents. He waved his red cape with a flourish and shouted, "Ole!" at the angry bull. This was the moment he'd been waiting for. All of his life, he had dreamed about being a matador. But when the bull charged, the man dropped his cape and went running across the arena. In a great leap, he cleared the wall. With the bull still snorting in the ring, the bullfighter decided that he would find something different to do with his life.

Moral:

_____

_____

3. A famous violinist named Joshua Bell played his violin at a subway stop in Washington, DC. Bell's violin is worth $3.5 million. In a concert hall, people pay $100 a seat to hear him play. But when Bell played in the subway station, nobody recognized him, nobody applauded, nobody cared. Only a few people stopped to listen before they moved on.

Moral:

_____

_____

4. A small toddler dressed in diapers wandered into a busy Boston street. None of the impatient drivers stopped to help the poor child, but kept going around him and beeping their horns at him. A mother saw this sickening spectacle from her car and rushed into the road, heedless of her own safety. She grabbed the toddler and carried him to safety. "That's how I would want other people to treat my kids," the mother explained.

Moral:

_____

_____

5. After an enormous blizzard in Washington, DC, the city sent out its powerful snow plows to clear the roads. But the snow was heaped so high that even the plows got stuck. Some of the plows had to be dug out by people carrying old-fashioned shovels.

Moral:

_____

_____

6. A taxi driver discovered that his last passenger had left a fat wallet in the back of his cab. In fact, the wallet was stuffed full of cash—nearly $6,000. Instead of stealing the money, the driver hurried back to the airport and handed the money over to his grateful passenger. "If the money doesn't belong to me, I don't keep it," the taxi driver said later. "I know that God is watching everybody every second."

Moral:

_____

_____

Lesson 9 ···

Summary— Crying Wolf

This next fable by Aesop is one of his most familiar, and it warns us about the dangers of lying. Like the expressions "sour grapes" and "belling the cat," **crying wolf** is used by modern people to convey an idea. See if you can guess what it means "to cry Wolf" by the way it is used in these sentences:

- You say you can't go to school because your tummy aches. I think you're crying wolf.
- Unless there's really a fire, don't ever yell, "Fire!" That's crying wolf.
- There's a robber in our backyard! I'm not crying wolf!

There's another warning in this story that is equally strong as the warning against lying. Let's see if we can discover what it is.

The Shepherd Boy and the Wolf

A Shepherd Boy tended his Master's sheep near a dark forest not far from the village. In a short while, he found life in the pasture very **dull**. "I'm so bored," he thought. "I have nothing to do to amuse myself except for talking to my dog. The sheep are not interesting at all. They chew grass with a stupid look all day long."

One day as the Shepherd Boy sat watching the sheep and the quiet forest, he thought up a plan to have some fun. His Master had told him to call for help should a Wolf attack the flock, and the Villagers would drive it away. So now, though he had not seen anything that even looked like a Wolf, he ran toward the village shouting, "Help! Wolf! Help!"

Just as he expected, the Villagers heard the cry and dropped their work, running in great excitement to the pasture. But when they got there, they found the Boy rolling on the ground. "I sure tricked you!" the Boy laughed. "Oh, that was a good joke!"

A few days later, the Shepherd Boy again shouted, "Wolf! Wolf!" The Villagers ran to help him, only to be laughed at again. "I got you twice!" the Boy laughed.

Then one evening as the sun was setting behind the forest, and the shadows of the forest were creeping over the pasture, a Wolf really did spring from the trees and fall upon the sheep. Its greedy teeth flashed in the gloom.

In terror, the Boy ran toward the village shouting, "Wolf! Help! Wolf!"

But though the Villagers heard the cry, they ignored it. "Wolf indeed!" they scoffed.

"Please help!" shouted the Boy. "I'm telling the truth! Wolf!"

But the Villagers said, "He cannot fool us again."

The Wolf killed a great many of the sheep and then slipped silently into the forest.

Tell It Back—Narration

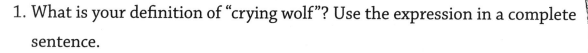

Without looking at the fable, tell back *The Shepherd Boy and the Wolf* as best as you remember it using your own words. Or record your telling of the fable and then play it back.

- Keep the events of the story in their proper order.
- Use a sprinkling of words from the fable, such as the word "dull."

Here's the first sentence to get you started:

A Shepherd Boy tended his Master's sheep near a dark forest not far from the village.

Talk About It—

1. What is your definition of "crying wolf"? Use the expression in a complete sentence.
2. What are some of the usual reasons people lie? Have you told a lie? Tell the story of why you did it.
3. The Shepherd Boy lied because he was bored. Do people get into trouble more when they are bored or idle? Why? What would be a good moral to warn against the dangers of idleness?
4. In 2009, a family called the police emergency line to report a terrible tragedy. They said that their six-year-old son might have been carried off by a large

Lesson 9: Summary—Crying Wolf

helium balloon in their backyard. The balloon went up in the air about 7,000 feet and travelled more than fifty miles. Military helicopters were sent to follow the balloon, but it was feared that the little boy had fallen out of the basket. Search and rescue teams patrolled the ground for his dead body. Later, it was discovered that the boy had been hiding in a cardboard box in a small attic above the garage. As it turns out, the parents had told the boy to hide. They had sent the balloon up in the air and called the police just to get attention from TV cameras. This incident is known as the "Balloon Boy Hoax." A hoax is a deliberate attempt to trick people. How is the "Balloon Boy Hoax" like the fable *The Shepherd Boy and the Wolf*? How is it different?

5. Look carefully at this painting by Elizabeth Jane Gardner entitled *The Shepherd David*. Is this Shepherd Boy like the Boy who cried wolf? Why or why not?

Go Deeper—

1. Circle the moral that works best for *The Shepherd Boy and the Wolf*:
   a. "Liars are not believed even when they speak the truth."
   b. "Avoid forests as night is falling."
   c. "Laughter makes work less boring."
   d. "Shepherd boys are never to be trusted."

2. Can you think of another moral for the fable? Write it in the space below.

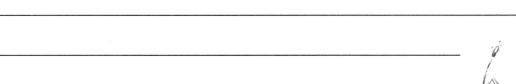

_____

_____

_____

3. Like many words, the adjective "dull" has more than one meaning.

It can mean that something is not bright or colorful:

The winter sky is very dull today.

It can mean thick-headed or stupid:

Cows are such dull beasts that they stand outside in the pouring rain.

It can mean that something is not sharp or keen:

My dull knife can't cut the string.

It can mean boring and uninteresting:

Watching TV is sometimes as dull as watching wet paint dry.

Because the Shepherd Boy has nobody to talk to or to play with, he feels that being at the pasture is very dull. The word "dull" in this sentence probably means (circle one):

    a. stupid   b. not sharp   c. boring   d. dim

Use the word "dull" in two sentences. Make sure your sentences give us a clue why something is dull.

Sample sentences: Khaki is a dull color.

    I have a dull ache in my tooth.

    The dull detective missed all the clues.

    The family video was quite dull.

a. _____

_____

b. _____

_____

4. What animals could replace a wolf and sheep and still have the fable make sense?

    a. a lobster and crabs

    b. a dog and puppies

    c. a frog and fish

    d. a lion and goats

5. In the Hebrew Scriptures, David spends his boyhood as a shepherd. He tells King Saul: "Your servant has been keeping his father's sheep. When a lion or a bear came and carried off a sheep from the flock, I went after it, struck it and rescued the sheep from its mouth. When it turned on me, I seized it by its hair, struck it, and killed it. Your servant has killed both the lion and the bear . . ." (1 Samuel 17:34-36).

What do you think was the most important job of a shepherd? Write a complete sentence.

_____

_____

_____

_____

6. Psalm 23—a famous biblical passage about a shepherd—gives us other clues about this job.

    ¹ The LORD is my shepherd, I shall not be in want.

      ² He makes me lie down in green pastures,

    he leads me beside quiet waters,

      ³ he restores my soul. (Psalm 23:1-3)

Based on this well-known passage, what was a shepherd expected to do for his sheep? Write a complete sentence.

_____

_____

_____

Writing Time

1. **COPYWORK**—In the space provided, neatly copy the following sentence:

   As the Shepherd Boy sat watching the sheep, he thought up a plan to have some fun.

   _____

   _____

   _____

   What two things are happening at the same time in this "as" sentence?

   _____

   _____

2. **DICTATION**—Your teacher will read to you about wolves. Please listen carefully! After your teacher reads once, she will read slowly again and include the punctuation marks. Your task will be to write down the sentences as your teacher reads them one by one.

   _____

   _____

   _____

   _____

   _____

   _____

   _____

   _____

Lesson 9: Summary—Crying Wolf

3. **SENTENCE PLAY**—"I'm so bored," the Shepherd Boy thought. "I have nothing to do to amuse myself except for talking to my dog." Using this sentence as a model, write two other sentences to show how bored the Shepherd Boy is.

"I have nothing to do to amuse myself except for _____."

a. _____

_____

_____

b. _____

_____

_____

c. What if the Shepherd Boy had said, "I'm so excited!" instead of "I'm so bored"? How would this change the thoughts that follow? Write a sentence.

"I'm so excited! I can _____."

_____

_____

_____

4. **COPIOUSNESS**

a. Write the definition of a noun and an adjective below.

A "noun" is a _____

_____.

An "adjective" _____

_____.

b. Mark the nouns and adjectives in the sentence below. Place an *N* over the nouns and an *ADJ* over the adjectives. There are three nouns and two adjectives.

A Shepherd Boy tended sheep near a dark forest.

c. Let's drop the adjective "dark" from the sentence and replace it with other adjectives that mean nearly the same thing (example: shadowy). Use a thesaurus only if you get stuck.

1) A Shepherd Boy tended sheep near a _____ forest.
(adjective for dark)

2) A Shepherd Boy tended sheep near a _____ forest.
(adjective for dark)

d. Rearrange and rewrite the sentence using a different subject. Keep the original meaning. Do you remember what a subject is?

A Shepherd Boy tended sheep near a dark forest.

Make sheep the subject of your sentence.

Sheep _____.

e. Try to find nouns that have nearly the same meaning to replace the underlined nouns in the following sentence:

The Villagers heard the cry and dropped their work, running in great excitement to the pasture.

_____

_____

_____

_____

_____

Lesson 9: Summary—Crying Wolf

5. <u>A Shepherd Boy tended his Master's sheep near a dark forest not far from the</u> <u>village</u>. Can you think of a scarier way to begin this fable? Remember that the forest contains wolves.

_____

_____

_____

_____

_____

6. **SUMMARY**—Here is the fable again. Read it once more and cross out any unnecessary sentences. Keep only the events, words, and dialogue which are important for communicating the main idea. You may also rewrite sentences to make them shorter.

The Shepherd Boy and the Wolf

A Shepherd Boy tended his Master's sheep near a dark forest not far from the village. In a short while, he found life in the pasture very dull. "I'm so bored," he thought. "I have nothing to do to amuse myself except for talking to my dog. The sheep are not interesting at all. They chew grass with a stupid look all day long."

One day as the Shepherd Boy sat watching the sheep and the quiet forest, he thought up a plan to have some fun. His Master had told him to call for help should a Wolf attack the flock, and the Villagers would drive it away. So now, though he had not seen anything that even looked like a Wolf, he ran toward the village shouting, "Help! Wolf! Help!"

Just as he expected, the Villagers heard the cry and dropped their work, running in great excitement to the pasture. But when they got there, they found the Boy rolling on the ground. "I sure tricked you!" the Boy laughed. "Oh, that was a good joke!"

A few days later, the Shepherd Boy again shouted, "Wolf! Wolf!" The Villagers ran to help him, only to be laughed at again. "I got you twice!" the Boy laughed.

Then one evening as the sun was setting behind the forest, and the shadows of the forest were creeping over the pasture, a Wolf really did spring from the trees and fall upon the sheep. Its greedy teeth flashed in the gloom.

In terror, the Boy ran toward the village shouting, "Wolf! Help! Wolf!"

But though the Villagers heard the cry, they ignored it. "Wolf indeed!" they scoffed.

"Please help!" shouted the Boy. "I'm telling the truth! Wolf!"

But the Villagers said, "He cannot fool us again."

The Wolf killed a great many of the sheep and then slipped silently into the forest.

SUMMARY

_____

_____

_____

_____

_____

_____

_____

_____

_____

_____

_____

_____

Lesson 9: Summary—Crying Wolf

_____

_____

_____

_____

_____

_____

_____

Speak It

Memorize your summary above and deliver it orally to your class, teacher, or recording device.[1] Everyone should count the number of words in his summary. Which classmate had the shortest number of words? Did that summary still make sense and support the moral, which is "Liars are not believed even when they speak the truth"?

---

1. To review elocution instructions, see page 143.

Lesson 10

Adding to a Fable— A Chinese Tale

Is this a good day or a bad day? Do you really know until the day is over? Say you find a lemon meringue pie in the refrigerator. That's good, isn't it? But then you eat the whole pie and get a stomachache. That's bad, isn't it? The stomachache causes you to stay home and you miss a trip to the dentist. That's good, isn't it? But then your tooth starts to really hurt. That's bad, isn't it?

Do you see the point? We often can't see circumstances clearly while we're in the middle of them. We may not know if something is good or bad until time passes.

This tale from China illustrates how things can turn out to be good or bad, but we don't necessarily know right away.

The Tale of the Chinese Farmer

Once there was a **prosperous** Farmer in China who owned a tall and strong Work Horse. During a lightning storm one night, the Horse broke out of his barn and ran away. The Farmer's Neighbors stopped by the Farmer's house to look at the broken barn door. "We are sorry for your bad day," the Neighbors said.

"How do you know it is a bad day?" the Farmer asked.

A few weeks later, the Horse returned to the Farmer's fields and it brought with it two beautiful wild horses. The Farmer's Neighbors stopped by the Farmer's house to cheer his good luck. "Three horses from one horse!" the Neighbors said. "This is a very good day."

"How do you know it is a good day?" the Farmer asked.

The next day, the Farmer's Son tried to catch one of the wild horses. The wild horse kicked him and broke the boy's leg. The Farmer's neighbors stopped by the Farmer's house to look at the poor boy's broken leg. "We're sorry for your bad day," the Neighbors said.

"How do you know it is a bad day?" the Farmer asked.

While the Farmer's Son was sick with pain and fever, a war broke out between two kings. Soldiers came to the Farmer's village and forced many young men and boys to join the army. The soldiers looked at the Farmer's Son, decided he was too sick to fight, and left him in bed. When the soldiers had left the village, the Farmer's Neighbors stopped by the Farmer's house to cheer his good luck. "Your Son is safe!" the Neighbors said. "This is a very good day."

"How do you know it is a good day?" the Farmer asked.

Do you see how this story could go on and on for a very long time? When something bad happens, something good follows. When something good happens, something bad follows. You will have a chance to add to this story.

Tell It Back—Narration

- Without looking at the fable, tell back *The Tale of the Chinese Farmer* as best as you can remember it using your own words. Remember that four things happen: two good things and two bad things. You can record your telling back for extra practice.
- Keep the events of the story in their proper order.

Here's the first sentence to get you started:

Once there was a <u>prosperous</u> Farmer in China who owned a tall and strong Work Horse.

Talk About It

1. Why doesn't the Chinese Farmer ever agree with his Neighbors that the day is good or bad?

2. How could you change this event to make it turn out to be a bad day?
   It was a good day! Tonya went for a ride on a roller coaster.

3. How could you change this event to make it turn out to be a good day?
   It was a bad day! Snow was coming down hard and Jason's football game was canceled.

Lesson 10: *Adding to a Fable—A Chinese Tale*

Go Deeper—

1. Choose the sentence that would make the best moral for this story:

    a. "Horses are troublesome animals."

    b. "Farmers have difficult lives."

    c. "Time must pass before we say something is good or bad."

    d. "Good things always follow bad things."

2. The word "<u>prosperous</u>" comes from the Latin word *prosperitatum*, which means "good fortune" or "success."

    Circle the best definition of <u>prosperous</u>.

    a. wealthy

    b. cheerful

    c. sick

    d. scared

    What clue do we have from the story that the Farmer is <u>prosperous</u>? Write a complete sentence.

    _____

    _____

    _____

3. Do you think the Farmer changes or remains the same? Give a reason for your answer.

    changes   remains the same

    _____

    _____

Writing Time—

1. **COPYWORK**—In the space provided, neatly copy the following sentence:

   While the Farmer's Son was sick with pain and fever, a war broke out between two kings.

   _____

   _____

   _____

   What two things are happening at the same time in this "while" sentence?

   _____

   _____

   _____

   _____

2. **DICTATION**—Your teacher will read to you about farmers. Please listen carefully! After your teacher reads once, she will read slowly again and include the punctuation marks. Your task will be to write down the sentences as your teacher reads them one by one.

   _____

   _____

   _____

   _____

   _____

_____

_____

_____

_____

_____

_____

3. **SENTENCE PLAY**—<u>When the soldiers left the village, the Farmer's Neighbors stopped by the Farmer's house</u>. Using this sentence as a model, write two other sentences to show what the Farmer's Neighbors did.

When the soldiers left the village, the Farmer's Neighbors _____."

a. _____

_____

_____

b. _____

_____

_____

c. Write a <u>when</u> sentence to show that when one thing happens, something else follows.

When _____

_____

_____

4. COPIOUSNESS

a. Mark the nouns and adjectives in the sentence below. Place an *N* over the nouns and an *ADJ* over the adjectives. There are three nouns and three adjectives. Remember that a noun is a person, place, thing, or idea. An adjective describes a noun.

During a storm, the horse broke out of his red, wooden barn.

b. Replace two of the adjectives in the sentence with any adjectives that make sense.

During a storm, the horse broke out of his _____,

_____ barn.

c. Now add a string of adjectives to describe the horse.

During a storm, the _____, _____,

_____, _____ horse broke out

of his red, wooden barn.

d. Replace the nouns in the sentence with any nouns that make sense.

During a _____, the _____

broke out of his red, wooden _____.

e. Rearrange and rewrite the sentence using a different subject. Keep the original meaning. Remember that the subject is what the sentence is about.

The Farmer's Son was kicked by the horse.

Make <u>horse</u> the subject of your sentence.

The horse _____

Boys were forced by soldiers to join the army.

Make <u>soldiers</u> the subject of your sentence.

Soldiers _____.

5. AMPLIFICATION BY EXTENSION

We are going to amplify *The Tale of the Chinese Farmer*. Instead of making the story longer with dialogue or description, we are going to add to the story by making something new happen. Do you remember what happened last?

> When the soldiers had left the village, the Farmer's Neighbors stopped by the Farmer's house to cheer his good luck. "Your Son is safe!" the Neighbors said. "This is a very good day."
> "How do you know it is a good day?" the Farmer asked.

Following the pattern of the story, whenever something bad happens, something good is supposed to follow.

Write a paragraph that shows something bad happening to the Farmer, the Farmer's family or his animals.

_____

_____

_____

_____

_____

_____

_____

_____

_____

_____

_____

_____

_____

_____

Speak It—

We are going to play a word game that replaces the nouns and adjectives in a short story. Most of the nouns and adjectives are left out of this story. One student asks other students for nouns and adjectives and writes down the answers in the blank spaces. When all the blanks have been filled, the student then reads the story out loud. Or the resulting story could also be recorded and played back. In either case, the result is usually pretty silly.

The Tale of the _____ Farmer
(adjective)

Once there was a prosperous Farmer in _____, who
(place noun)

owned a _____ and _____ horse.
      (adjective)   (adjective)

During a lightning storm one _____, the horse broke out of
     (noun)

his _____ and ran away. The Farmer's Neighbors stopped by the
   (noun)

Farmer's _____ to look at the broken _____. "We
     (noun)   (noun)

are sorry for your _____ day," the Neighbors said.
     (adjective)

"How do you know it is a _____ day?" the Farmer asked.
(same adjective as before)

A few weeks later, the horse returned to the Farmer's fields and it brought with

it _____ wild _____. The Farmer's Neighbors
   (big number)   (plural noun)

stopped by the Farmer's house to cheer his good _____.
                                                        (noun)

"_____ _____ from one horse!" the Neighbors
  (same big number)   (same plural noun)

said. "This is a very good _____."
                                 (noun)

"How do you know?" the Farmer asked.

Lesson 11

Following an Outline

Aesop is given credit for nearly all the fables in this book so far. But Aesop was not the only writer of fables. We've also read a fable from India, *The Hunter and the Doves*, and a fable by Jean de la Fontaine, *The Partridge and the Hare*. Two short fables appear in the Hebrew Scriptures, one in the book of Judges (next page) and another in 2 Kings 14:9. *The Trees Choose a King* may be the oldest fable on record anywhere, and it might have been written by the last judge of Israel, Samuel.

This fable mentions the cedars of Lebanon. These trees are stout, beautiful trees found in the mountains of Lebanon, Turkey, and Syria. Once they grew over 100 feet tall, but there are only a few old cedars left today.

The Trees Choose a King

One day, the Trees went out to **anoint** a King for themselves. They said to the Olive Tree, "Be our King."

But the Olive Tree answered, "Should I give up my oil, by which both gods and men are honored, to hold sway[1] over the Trees?"

Next, the Trees said to the Fig Tree, "Come and be our King."

But the Fig Tree replied, "Should I give up my fruit, so good and sweet, to hold sway over the Trees?"

Then the Trees said to the [Grape] Vine, "Come and be our King."

But the Vine answered, "Should I give up my wine, which cheers both gods and men, to hold sway over the Trees?"

Finally, the Trees said to the Thornbush, "Come and be our King."

The Thornbush said to the Trees, "If you really want to anoint me King over you, come and take refuge in my shade; but if not, then let fire come out of the Thornbush and consume the Cedars of Lebanon!"

—adapted from Judges 9:8-15

1. Please note that the words "hold sway" can be simplified as the word "rule."

Tell It Back—Narration

Without looking at the fable, tell back *The Trees Choose a King* as best as you remember it using your own words. Remember that three useful plants are asked to be King: an Olive Tree, a Fig Tree, and a Grape Vine. They all refuse. For extra practice, you can record your telling back.

- Keep the events of the story in their proper order.
- Use a sprinkling of words from the fable, such as the word "anoint."

Here's the first sentence to get you started:

One day, the Trees went out to anoint a King for themselves. They said to the Olive Tree, "Be our King."

Talk About It—

1. At first, the Trees go to worthy trees and plants to ask them to be King. Why do you suppose the worthy trees refuse?

2. The Trees can only get a worthless Thornbush to agree to be King. Why do you suppose the Thornbush agrees? What does the Thornbush mean by "let fire come out of the Thornbush"? What are the dangers in having a worthless person be King?

3. Were the Trees wise or foolish to keep looking for a King once the worthy trees had refused?

4. Look carefully at these two paintings: *Olive Trees with Yellow Sky and Sun* by Vincent van Gogh (left) and *Grove of Olive Trees in Bordighera* by Claude Monet (right). Which artist makes the trees look more important? Why do you think so?

Lesson 11: *Following an Outline*

Go Deeper—

1. Psalm 23:5 says, "You anoint my head with oil." From this clue, write your own definition for the word "anoint."

   To anoint means to _____

   _____

   _____

   _____

2. The book of Proverbs is full of warnings against foolish and evil kings. Which of these proverbs would make the best moral for this fable?

   a. "Love and faithfulness keep a king safe . . ." (Proverbs 20:28).

   b. "If a king judges the poor with fairness, his throne will always be secure" (Proverbs 29:14).

   c. "When the wicked rule, the people groan" (Proverbs 29:2).

   d. "He who tends a fig tree will eat its fruit" (Proverbs 27:18).

3. Which of the following titles would best fit this fable?

   a. The Wonderful Thornbush

   b. The Olive Tree Refuses to Be King

   c. A Good King for the Trees

   d. A Bad King for the Trees

Writing Time—

1. **COPYWORK**—In the space provided, neatly copy the following sentence:

   They said to the Olive Tree, "Be our King."

   _____

   _____

   _____

The sentence above contains dialogue. We know that the Trees are talking because quotation marks surround what is being said. What if the other Trees complimented the Olive Tree's beautiful fruit? Use quotation marks to create new dialogue.

They said to the Olive Tree, "_____."

_____

_____

_____

_____

2. **DICTATION**—Your teacher will read to you about fig trees. Please listen carefully! After your teacher reads once, he will read slowly again and include the punctuation marks. Your task will be to write down the sentences as your teacher reads them one by one.

_____

_____

_____

_____

_____

_____

_____

_____

_____

_____

Lesson 11: *Following an Outline*

3. **SENTENCE PLAY**—<u>The Fig Tree replied, "Should I give up my fruit, so good and sweet, to hold sway over the Trees?"</u> What if a different sort of Tree talked? What would it say?

a. Using the following sentence as a model, write a sentence of dialogue to show what a Nut Tree would say about its nuts.

The _____ Tree replied, "Should I give up my _____,

so _____ and _____,

to rule over the Trees?"

b. Now write a sentence of dialogue with a Peach Tree talking.

_____

_____

_____

c. Now write a sentence of dialogue with a Chewing Gum Tree talking.

_____

_____

_____

4. Using the fable *The Trees Choose a King* as a model, <u>write</u> your own fable using animals instead of trees. Remember to start with three worthy animals. Each animal refuses to become King because he doesn't want to give up his special gifts. Finally, the animals find a worthless animal that agrees to become King as long as he can harm his subjects.

Ask yourself:
- What <u>worthy animal</u> would make a gifted ruler?
- What <u>worthless animal</u> would want power over the other animals?

The Animals Choose a King [or Queen]

One day, the Animals went out to anoint a King [or Queen] for themselves . . .

_____

_____

_____

_____

_____

_____

_____

_____

_____

_____

_____

_____

_____

_____

MORAL _____

_____

Speak It—

- Read your fable to your class and teacher or record your fable and play it back.
- Do your classmates think that your moral fits well with your fable?

Lesson 12

My Own Fable, Part 1

Today you are going to pretend to be Aesop. The purpose of this lesson is to write a fable from scratch!

Remember:

- Your fable should use animals that act and talk like people.
- Your fable should teach a lesson.
- Your fable should have a moral at the end that makes the lesson clear.

Go Deeper—

Before you can write a fable, you need to think about what types of animals to use. Every character in a story, whether animal or human, has certain character traits. What is a "character trait"? It is anything that stands out about a character. We learn about character traits through thoughts, words, and actions.

For example, we think of a peacock as proud, don't we? Pride is the main character trait of peacocks. How did people come to think of peacocks as proud?

It's not that peacocks are really any prouder than other birds, as if any bird can be proud in a human sense. But it is true that the male peacock has the fanciest feathers of any bird in the world and walks very grandly. If a boy always got dressed up in his fanciest clothes and strutted around for everyone to see, we would certainly think of him as proud. Storytellers give animals the character traits that people would imagine them to have if they were human. Over the centuries, many stories have been told about peacocks and their pride. Now it's hard not to imagine peacocks without thinking of pride. Any person who shows off her clothing and struts around is being "as proud as a peacock."

What do we think of a donkey? After reading *The Ass and His Driver*, most people would say the word that best describes a donkey is "stupid." It's not that donkeys are really stupider than horses, llamas, or camels. Storytellers have given donkeys the character trait of stupidity. In fables, a donkey often takes the place of a stupid or stubborn person.

When you write your fable, you will need to choose animals that display the character traits of a person. For instance, a gorilla can take the place of a bully. A pig can take the place of a slob. A lamb can take the place of an innocent. Let's have some practice with the exercises in this lesson.

1. Using the adjectives below, see if you can choose the typical <u>character trait</u> to describe the following animals.

<u>Adjectives:</u>

silly   brave   quiet   angry   gentle   dirty

   hungry   wise   sly   strong   busy

Fox   _____

Rat   _____

Lion   _____

Wolf   _____

Lesson 12: My Own Fable, Part 1

Goose _____

Lamb _____

Owl _____

Mouse _____

Bull _____

Ox _____

Bee _____

2. Make up your own adjectives to describe the animals below.

Bear _____

Cat _____

Dog _____

Spider _____

Rooster _____

Besides choosing animals for your fable, you will need to have a moral lesson to teach. What lesson do you think needs to be taught? Here are some possibilities:

- "Be kind to your neighbor."
- "Don't listen to gossip."
- "Obey your parents."
- "Love your enemy."
- "Think before you act."
- "Always tell the truth."
- "Never trust an evildoer."
- "Avoid trouble when possible."
- "A good night's sleep improves the day."
- "Hard work pays off."

3. Which set of animals would work best for a lesson in <u>loving your enemy</u>?

   a. a mouse and a cat

   b. a bull and a cow

   c. a duck and a goose

   d. a frog and a turtle

4. Which set of animals would work best for a lesson in <u>obeying your parents</u>?

   a. a rooster and a fox

   b. a duck and ducklings

   c. a crow and a sparrow

   d. a spider and a fly

5. Which set of animals would work best for a lesson in <u>avoiding trouble</u>?

   a. a lion and a flea

   b. a horse and a camel

   c. a cow and a calf

   d. a pig and a skunk

Imitation

The moral of my fable will be:

_____

_____

The animals I use will be:

1. _____ to illustrate the character trait of

_____.

2. _____ to illustrate the character trait of

_____.

TITLE _____

<u>Hint</u>—Most fable titles are very simple. They name the animals in the story.

Lesson 12: My Own Fable, Part 1

_____

_____

_____

_____

_____

_____

_____

_____

_____

_____

_____

_____

_____

_____

_____

_____

_____

_____

_____

MORAL _____

_____

Speak It—

Here's a fun **rhyme** to memorize about common traits given to animals and other objects. Poems that rhyme are especially easy to learn because one sound leads to another. Remember to break the poem up into smaller sections (called **stanzas**) and learn each section before moving on. Remember to see the elocution instructions on page 143. Consider reading the poem aloud and recording it to play it back and help you to learn it through repetition.

Old Sayings

As poor as a church mouse, As thin as a rail,
As fat as a porpoise, As rough as a gale,
As brave as a lion, As spry as a cat,
As bright as a sixpence, As weak as a rat.

As proud as a peacock, As sly as a fox,
As mad as a March hare, As strong as an ox,
As fair as a lily, As empty as air,
As rich as was Croesus, As cross as a bear.

As pure as an angel, As neat as a pin,
As smart as a steel trap, As ugly as sin.
As dead as a door nail, As white as a sheet,
As flat as a pancake, As red as a beet.

As round as an apple, As black as your hat,
As brown as a berry, As blind as a bat,
As mean as a miser, As full as a tick,
As plump as a partridge, As sharp as a stick.

As clean as a penny, As dark as a pall,
As hard as a millstone, As bitter as gall,
As fine as a fiddle, As clear as a bell,
As dry as a herring, As deep as a well.

As light as a feather, As hard as a rock,
As stiff as a poker, As calm as a clock,
As green as a goblin, As brisk as a bee,
And now let me stop, Lest you weary of me.

From *Chance Hits* [1915] by Norman H. Chance

Lesson 12: *My Own Fable, Part 1*

Lesson 13 ·······································

My Own Fable, Part 2

Start with a Moral

Let's say you were given a simple moral—"A shy cat makes a proud mouse." Would you be able to write a fable to go along with that? First of all, you'd need to know what the moral means. "A shy cat makes a proud mouse" is another way of saying that "A weakling becomes prideful when the strong are fearful." The situation and the characters are ready-made. You would write a story about a Mouse who boasts and swaggers around a "fraidy" Cat. "Fetch me some of your cat food," the Mouse might say, "and don't twitch your whiskers at me. And after I eat your food, I want you to scratch my back."

What if you were given a more general moral without the ready-made situation? For instance—"When pride comes, then comes disgrace." Again, the first step to writing a fable is to understand the moral. This moral means that pride (or arrogance) makes a person foolish, and it's only a matter of time before he does something disgraceful or dangerous. Here's another way to put it—"Pride goes before a fall." How would you illustrate such a moral? Well, you could tell about the same Mouse in the first moral, only this time he boasts about being brave around a Baby Kitten. When the Mother Cat returns to her lair, what happens? The proud Mouse is eaten in a single bite.

After creating a fable from scratch, it should not be too hard for you to invent your own fable from a moral. Think of the moral as the springboard at a swimming pool. Jump off the moral and dive into the deep end of your own ideas.

Talk About It—

Let's start by telling a story out loud. Your teacher will give you a moral. Think about what the moral means and how you might illustrate it with characters. If your teacher wants, you and your classmates can tell the story sentence by sentence, round-robin style around the room. You could also record the story and play it back. Feel free to use stories you already know, such as fairy tales, to illustrate the moral.

Here are some ideas:

- "A fair face may hide a foul heart."

For this moral, the fair face could be a Green Emerald Snake that lures a Mouse into a hug of death. Can you think of another deadly animal with a fair face?

Or you could simply tell the story of Snow White's wicked, but beautiful, Stepmother.

Here's another moral:

- "A fall into a ditch makes you wiser."

Here's a story for this moral: A Porcupine wants to touch the moon, and so he climbs higher and higher in a tree to reach it. A gust of wind causes him to tumble down into a water-filled ditch.

Can you think of another foolish animal that learns a lesson by falling?

Here are some other morals to think about. What characters might illustrate these morals:

- *A large fire starts with a small spark.*
- *A lazy Sheep thinks its own wool is heavy.*
- *A Leopard cannot change his spots.*

Writing Time—

In this section, you will be trying your hand at writing a brief story to illustrate one or more of the following morals. After each of the following morals/proverbs, write down what you think is the meaning of the moral/proverb, and then think of a situation and the animal characters to go along with it. Some of the morals lend themselves easily to situations. Others are more general.

1. *"If many people dread you, then beware of many people."*—Ausonius
   - What is the <u>meaning</u> of this moral/proverb?

   _____

   _____

   - What situation and characters would help to illustrate this moral?

   _____

   _____

2. *A cake eaten in peace is worth two in trouble.*
   - What is the <u>meaning</u> of the above moral/proverb?

   _____

   _____

   - What situation and characters would help to illustrate this moral?

   _____

   _____

3. *The cure is sometimes worse than the sickness.*

　　● What is the <u>meaning</u> of the above moral/proverb?

_____

_____

　　● What situation and characters would help to illustrate this moral?

_____

_____

_____

4. *A closed mouth catches no flies.*

　　● What is the <u>meaning</u> of the above moral/proverb?

_____

_____

　　● What situation and characters would help to illustrate this moral?

_____

_____

_____

5. *Slow help is no help.*

　　● What is the <u>meaning</u> of the above moral/proverb?

_____

_____

　　● What situation and characters would help to illustrate this moral?

_____

_____

　　　　　　　Lesson 13: *My Own Fable, Part 2*

6. *Spit not in the well. You may have to drink its water.*

   ● What is the <u>meaning</u> of the above moral/proverb?

_____

_____

   ● What situation and characters would help to illustrate this moral?

_____

_____

_____

7. *We would be sorry if we got everything we wanted.*

   ● What is the <u>meaning</u> of the above moral/proverb?

_____

_____

   ● What situation and characters would help to illustrate this moral?

_____

_____

_____

Write a brief fable to illustrate one or more of the morals in the preceding section.

_____

_____

_____

_____

_____

_____

Lesson 13: My Own Fable, Part 2

Lesson 13: *My Own Fable, Part 2*

Lesson 14

Changing Point of View

All of the fables in this book have been told in a **third-person point of view**. That means that the fable writer acts like an onlooker or a reporter, watching things happen and then recording the action. Have you ever watched two people quarrel? Or dance? Or play a duet on the piano? You are the third person, watching the action, but not participating in the action. You can tell "third-person voice" when you see the words "he," "she," "it," and "they."

- Remember the clever Crow? "She gathered a pile of small pebbles."
- Remember the not-so-clever Ass? "He tumbled head over heels down the mountainside."

"He," "she," "it," and "they" are all third-person point of view.

None of our fables has been told in **first-person point of view**. First person uses the words "I," "me," and "my." When a storyteller uses the words "I," "me," and "my," what happens? The story becomes more personal. It's all about what one person is thinking and doing.

- I gathered a pile of pebbles until my mouth was dry.
- I tumbled head over heels down the mountainside. My whole body ached with bruises.

Do you see? We get a better idea of what the character is thinking inside her head.

We are going to read another famous fable by Aesop, *The Ants and the Grasshopper*, which is told in third person. Afterwards, we are going to experiment with changing the view to first person.

The Ants and the Grasshopper

One bright day in late autumn, a family of Ants was bustling about in the warm sunshine, drying out the grain they had stored up during the summer, when a starving Grasshopper, his fiddle under his arm, came up and humbly begged for a bite to eat.

"What!" cried the Ants in surprise. "Haven't you stored anything away for the winter? What in the world were you doing all last summer?"

"I didn't have time to store up any food," whined the Grasshopper. "I was so busy making sweet music that before I knew it the summer was gone."

Lesson 14: *Changing Point of View*

The Ants shrugged their shoulders in **disgust**. "Making music, were you?" they cried. "Very well; now dance!" And they turned their backs on the Grasshopper and went on with their work.

MORAL: *There's a time for work and a time for play.*

Tell It Back—Narration

- Without looking at the fable, tell back *The Ants and the Grasshopper* as best as you remember it using your own words. You could also record it on your favorite device and play it back.
  - Keep the events of the story in their proper order.
  - Use a sprinkling of words from the fable, such as the word "disgust."

Here's part of the first sentence to get you started:

One bright day in late autumn, a family of Ants was bustling about in the warm sunshine, drying out the grain they had stored up during the summer.

Talk About It—

1. Have you ever done a job with a brother, sister, or classmate and felt that this person did not work as hard as you did? How did you feel?

2. Do you have any chores to do at home? Why do you suppose your parents make you work around the house? What would happen if nobody in your family did the work?

3. How are ants and grasshoppers similar? How are they different?

4. In 1607, a few boats carrying Englishmen landed in America. They set up a fort in the wild woods of Virginia on the banks of the James River. Some of the settlers had come seeking gold and they knew very little about farming. They were happy to eat little scraps of food as long as they didn't have to work very hard. The leader of the settlers, Captain John Smith, realized that the whole fort would die of starvation if the people kept looking for gold instead of farming. He said to them, "He who works not, eats not." In other words, "If you don't work, you don't eat!" Even though John Smith did his best, the settlement of

Jamestown went through a terrible starving time in the winter of 1609-1610. How is this story similar to and different from *The Ants and the Grasshopper*?

Go Deeper—

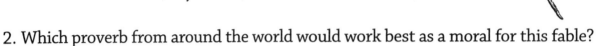

1. What might be another title for this fable, *The Ants and the Grasshopper*?

    a. Music Is a Waste of Time

    b. The Lazy Grasshopper

    c. The Greedy Ants

    d. Summertime Is Playtime

2. Which proverb from around the world would work best as a moral for this fable?

    a. "Smiling will gain you ten years of life."—Chinese

    b. "As a man works, so he eats."—German

    c. "The grass is greener on the other side of the fence."—English

    d. "Wash your hands, and you can eat with kings."—African

3. Which set of animals below could replace the Ants and the Grasshopper and still have the moral make sense? Remember that the Ants are hard workers and the Grasshopper is lazy.

    a. wolves and a deer

    b. flies and a spider

    c. cats and a kitten

    d. honeybees and a butterfly

4. The word "disgust" is a combined word that comes from the Latin prefix *dis*, which means "opposite of," and the Latin verb *gustare*, which means "to taste." We have other words in English, besides disgust, that are derived from *gustare*, such as "gustatory" (meaning good tasting) and "gusto" (meaning enjoyment). What do you think is the meaning of the word "disgust"? What are some other "dis" words that could replace the word "disgust"? Circle the words that make sense to you, but you must be able to defend your answer.

Lesson 14: *Changing Point of View*

The Ants shrugged their shoulders in <u>disgust</u>.

a. dislike

b. disagreement

c. distaste

d. disappearance

e. disbelief

f. disobedience

g. discovery

h. disapproval

Use the noun "<u>disgust</u>" in your own complete sentence.

_____

_____

Use the adjective "disgusting" in your own complete sentence.

_____

_____

Writing Time—

1. **COPYWORK**—Neatly copy the sentence in the space provided:

"I didn't have time to store up any food," whined the Grasshopper.

_____

_____

_____

_____

_____

The sentence above contains dialogue. We know that the Grasshopper is talking because quotation marks surround what is being said. What else could the Grasshopper whine about? (Think about the chilly autumn weather or his sore feet or his growling stomach.) Use quotation marks to create new dialogue.

"_____," whined the Grasshopper.

_____

_____

_____

2. **DICTATION**—Your teacher will read to you about grasshoppers. Please listen carefully! After your teacher reads once, he will read slowly again and include the punctuation marks. Your task will be to write down the sentences as your teacher reads them one by one.

_____

_____

_____

_____

_____

_____

_____

Lesson 14: Changing Point of View

3. **SENTENCE PLAY**—Often, long sentences can be split up to make smaller sentences. Carefully read this long sentence:

One bright day in late autumn, a family of Ants was bustling about in the warm sunshine, drying out the grain they had stored up during the summer, when a starving Grasshopper, his fiddle under his arm, came up and humbly begged for a bite to eat.

a. Delete the word "when." Now divide the long sentence up into two complete sentences:

_____

_____

_____

_____

b. Try to divide the sentence up into four complete sentences:

_____

_____

_____

_____

_____

_____

c. <u>What in the world were you doing all last summer?</u> Using this sentence as a model, replace the question "what" with the words "why" and "how." Now ask the Grasshopper about his laziness.

Example: <u>Why</u> in the world did you think you could make music all summer?

<u>Why</u> in the world _____

_____

<u>How</u> in the world _____

_____

4. **COPIOUSNESS**—Mark the nouns and adjectives in the sentence below. Place an *N* over the nouns and an *ADJ* over the adjective. There are four nouns and one adjective.

"I was so busy making sweet music that before I knew it the summer was gone."

a. In the following sentence, replace the nouns and adjective with **synonyms**. A synonym is a word that has nearly the same meaning as another word. Some noun synonyms for "music" might be "song" or "tune."

I was so busy making _____ _____
                                     (adjective for sweet)   (noun for music)

that before I knew it _____ was gone.
                              (summer month noun)

b. Replace the nouns and adjective with any words that make sense.

I was so busy making _____ _____
                                    (adjective)   (noun)

that before I knew it the _____ was gone.
                              (noun)

5. **REWRITE**—Your teacher will divide up the classroom. Half of your classmates will rewrite the story in first-person point of view (I), as if they are playing the part of the lazy Grasshopper. Half of your classmates will rewrite the story in first-person point of view (I), as if they are playing the part of a hard-working Ant. Feel free to amplify the fable to make it longer.

Lesson 14: *Changing Point of View*

The Ants and the Grasshopper

One bright day in late autumn, a family of Ants was bustling about in the warm sunshine, drying out the grain they had stored up during the summer, when a starving Grasshopper, his fiddle under his arm, came up and humbly begged for a bite to eat.

"What!" cried the Ants in surprise. "Haven't you stored anything away for the winter? What in the world were you doing all last summer?"

"I didn't have time to store up any food," whined the Grasshopper. "I was so busy making sweet music that before I knew it the summer was gone."

The Ants shrugged their shoulders in disgust. "Making music, were you?" they cried. "Very well; now dance!" And they turned their backs on the Grasshopper and went on with their work.

MORAL: *There's a time for work and a time for play.*

_____

_____

_____

_____

_____

_____

_____

_____

_____

_____

_____

_____

Speak It—

Read your fable to your class, teacher, or recording device. How does the change in point of view from third person to first person make the fable different? Which view do you like better? Which view sounds as though you're right there in the story? Which view sounds fairer to both the Grasshopper and the Ants? Which view does the better job in illustrating the moral?

How does the telling of the story through the eyes of the Grasshopper change your feelings about him?

Lesson 14: *Changing Point of View*

Elocution Instructions

Whether you are reciting a poem or reading a story out loud, you want to speak in such a way that the audience can hear you <u>loud and clear</u>. The art of speaking skillfully is known as elocution. So, what goes into proper elocution?

First of all, you should make sure you are <u>pronouncing all of your words clearly</u>. This means you are making each word sharp and crisp instead of blending them together and mumbling. You want to say, "Betty eats butter better on bread," with each word separate from the next. You don't want to say, "Bettyeatsbutterbetteronbread."

Secondly, <u>good posture</u> is very important for speaking loudly enough. You can't breathe very well if you are slouched over. Stand up straight and tall, square your shoulders and look at your audience. <u>Look directly into their eyes</u>. This will help your listeners know that you are a confident speaker. They will enjoy your recitation more when they see how confident you are.

Finally, don't speak too quickly. It's hard to understand a recitation that blasts off like a rocket ship. You will want to <u>speak at a good pace</u> and pause every now and then to let your words sink in.

You will delight your listeners if you can stand up straight, look into their eyes, and speak loud and clear at just the right pace.

Glossary of New Words in This Book

New Concepts

Adjective—describes a noun and helps us to "see" it more clearly: e.g., happy, silly, strange

Amplification—a longer and more detailed version of a shorter story

Anthropomorphism—a storybook animal that acts like a human being

Copiousness—stretching exercises for students of rhetoric whereby students reach for new words to express variations of the same idea

Fable—a short story meant to teach a moral lesson

First Person—uses the pronouns "I," "me," "my"; the narrator takes part in the story

Memorize—to learn something by heart

Moral—the short lesson that explains the meaning of a fable

Noun—a person, place, thing, or idea: e.g., astronaut, island, sled, love

Point of View—a way of seeing things

Proverb—a wise saying

Rhyme—similar sounds repeated close to each other in poetry

Stanza—a section of poetry similar to a paragraph in prose

Subject—what the sentence is about

Summary—a shortened or concise version of a longer story

Synonym—a word that has nearly the same meaning as another word

Third Person—uses the pronouns "he," "she," "it," "one," "they"/"him," "her," "it," "one," "them"/"his," "her," "its," "one's," "their"

Vocabulary—a collection of words

Vocabulary Builder

Anoint—to apply oil, usually on the head of a new king or priest

Despise—to regard with contempt or dislike

Disaster—a terrible misfortune or a total failure

Disgust—a feeling of sickness or strong dislike

Dread—fear

Dull—boring, not colorful, stupid, or lacking sharpness

Lofty—high

Relish—enjoyment or zest

Prosperous—wealthy

Timid—shy

Vicious—evil or cruel

Willful—unreasonably stubborn

Expressions

Belling the Cat (see lesson 6)

Crying wolf (see lesson 9)

Sour grapes (see lesson 4)

Good-bye for Now—

Can it be that we must say farewell? Parting is such sweet sorrow. I trust that you enjoyed learning about fables.

But what exactly did you learn? Well, let's think for a moment.

You learned that fables are fabulous stories for teaching moral lessons. It's much easier to hear a fable than to suffer through a long lecture about being good.

But wait, there's more! You've learned to recognize two parts of speech: nouns and adjectives. A noun is a person, place, thing, or idea. An adjective describes a noun to help us see it more clearly. If you recognize these types of words, you can improve your skills in building happier, stronger, more sparkling sentences. Don't forget that most words—nouns and adjectives included—have synonyms. Synonyms are words that mean nearly the same thing as another word and they are extremely helpful in learning to write copiously.

Are we done yet? Allow me to remind you of summary and amplification. You have learned how to grow a story longer as well as shrink a story down. Summary is the shortening of a story to the most important details. Amplification is adding details to a story to make it longer and richer.

Alas, our moment is over. Now it is truly time to say good-bye. Good-bye and au revoir, auf Wiedersehen, *zai jian*, *sayonara*, shalom, adios, *kwaheri*, and *do svidaniya*!

Until we meet again—

See you back soon for *Writing & Rhetoric: Narrative I*, the next book in this series!

Notes

Notes

Notes

Notes

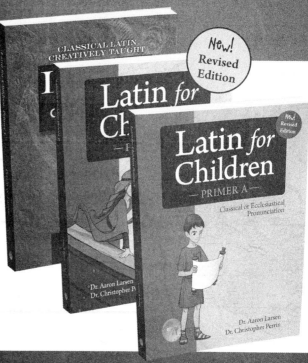

What are the best books your K–12 students should be reading?

Find out at:
ClassicalReader.com

Sort by grade, level, genre, and more!